Cambridge Elements ≡

Elements in Chinese Economy and Governance
edited by
Luke Qi Zhang
Fudan University
Mingxing Liu
Peking University
Daniel Mattingly
Yale University

ELITE CONFLICTS AND THE PATH TO ECONOMIC DECENTRALIZATION

Dong Zhang
The Hong Kong University of Science and Technology

Mingxing Liu
Peking University

Victor Shih
University of California at San Diego

CAMBRIDGE
UNIVERSITY PRESS

Shaftesbury Road, Cambridge CB2 8EA, United Kingdom

One Liberty Plaza, 20th Floor, New York, NY 10006, USA

477 Williamstown Road, Port Melbourne, VIC 3207, Australia

314–321, 3rd Floor, Plot 3, Splendor Forum, Jasola District Centre, New Delhi – 110025, India

103 Penang Road, #05–06/07, Visioncrest Commercial, Singapore 238467

Cambridge University Press is part of Cambridge University Press & Assessment, a department of the University of Cambridge.

We share the University's mission to contribute to society through the pursuit of education, learning and research at the highest international levels of excellence.

www.cambridge.org
Information on this title: www.cambridge.org/9781009544801

DOI: 10.1017/9781009544764

First published 2025

A catalogue record for this publication is available from the British Library.

ISBN 978-1-009-54480-1 Hardback
ISBN 978-1-009-54478-8 Paperback
ISSN 2976-5625 (online)
ISSN 2976-5617 (print)

Cambridge University Press & Assessment has no responsibility for the persistence or accuracy of URLs for external or third-party internet websites referred to in this publication and does not guarantee that any content on such websites is, or will remain, accurate or appropriate.

Elite Conflicts and the Path to Economic Decentralization

Elements in Chinese Economy and Governance

DOI: 10.1017/9781009544764
First published online: January 2025

Dong Zhang
The Hong Kong University of Science and Technology
Mingxing Liu
Peking University
Victor Shih
University of California at San Diego

Author for correspondence: Dong Zhang, dongzhang@ust.hk

Abstract: Why would a politically centralized state embark on the path of economic decentralization? This Element delves into the political origin of the puzzling economic decentralization in mainland China. The authors contend that the intra-elite conflicts between the authoritarian ruler and the ruling elites within the state prompted the ruler to pursue decentralization as a strategy to curb the influence wielded by the ruling elites. By examining the composition of the Chinese Communist Party's Central Committee, they find that the Cultural Revolution, fueled by elite conflicts, shifted the elite selectorate's composition from favoring central agencies to favoring local interests. Subsequent low turnover reinforced this shift, aligning elite incentives with decentralization policies and committing the Chinese leadership to a path of decentralization in the 1980s. Additionally, Taiwan's economic liberalization under the Kuomintang's authoritarian rule provides further evidence of the link between ruling party elite composition and economic policy orientation.

Keywords: economic decentralization, authoritarian regimes, ruling party, elite politics

ISBNs: 9781009544801 (HB), 9781009544788 (PB), 9781009544764 (OC)
ISSNs: 2976-5625 (online), 2976-5617 (print)

Contents

1 Introduction

Between the 1970s and 1990s, a highly unanticipated sequence of developments unfolded in the People's Republic of China. The Chinese Communist Party (CCP) initiated what has been termed "market-preserving federalism," devolving fiscal and regulatory authorities from the central to local governments, thereby to some extent constraining the interventionist role of the central government (Montinola, Qian, and Weingast, 1995; Qian and Roland, 1998; Qian and Weingast, 1997). The initiation of economic decentralization sparked the blossoming of private businesses in certain regions, which fueled over two decades of spectacular growth in these regions. Scholars have uncovered ample evidence that fiscal decentralization served as a pillar for China's remarkable growth from the 1970s to the 1990s (e.g., Oi, 1992; Qian, 2000; Xu, 2011).

Indeed, the Chinese-style "market-preserving federalism" presents a puzzle. In the wake of prolonged violent revolutions and warfare, the CCP eventually established a strong and centralized party-state in China by the middle of the twentieth century (Levitsky and Way, 2022). Given the entrenched interests of political elites within the central state and party machinery, it would seem unlikely for China to set a course toward economic decentralization. In a one-party dictatorship like the CCP, with its strict party hierarchy and top-down control system, one might expect pronounced predatory behavior from the central government, inherently placing local economic autonomy at risk and leaving it vulnerable to potential encroachment (Cai and Treisman, 2006, p. 506). Considering economic decentralization's integral role in China's growth miracle, a more fundamental question remains unanswered: In a highly centralized party-state such as China, what factors have steered the country on a path toward economic decentralization? And closely related, what mechanisms have ensured the sustainability of decentralization for a longer period?

The answers to these questions contribute to the understanding of China's economic miracle. We suggest that the political foundation of decentralization from the 1970s to the 1990s was not simply a result of top-down decentralization policies enacted by pro-reform elites in the late 1970s. In other words, economic decentralization is not equivalent to the "reform and opening up" policy typically conceived of by the general public. Rather, the Cultural Revolution, launched by Mao in 1966, in effect eradicated most of the central officials from the ruling elite in the Central Committee, thus paving the way for the enactment and persistence of decentralization policies throughout the 1980s and into the 1990s. We further demonstrate the reversal of this logic as central officials began to constitute a larger segment of the ruling elite in the

Central Committee during the 1990s. This shift in political power dynamics set the stage for a centralizing tendency in China's current growth model. In a sense, Mao's attempt to restore a utopian vision of communism through the Cultural Revolution unexpectedly paved the way for economic decentralization and a transition toward capitalism. The weakening of the central bureaucracy and the emergence of a leadership structure dominated by local elites during the Cultural Revolution in fact facilitated a shift toward the very economic system it aimed to oppose. This unintended consequence illustrates how agents' efforts to change institutions in pursuit of specific goals can trigger a complex interplay of factors that reshape the entire system, often leading to outcomes that diverge from their original intentions (e.g., Pierson, 2004). The economic decentralization following the Cultural Revolution stands as a striking example of how seemingly unrelated events can be connected in unexpected ways. The lesson for countries in the course of transitioning from statism to market economies is that broad objectives of economic reform do not necessarily translate into a unique blueprint plan, and that different contexts require tailored policy solutions to address context-specific constraints for economic development (Rodrik, 2006).

This Element aims to elucidate the political logic behind the implementation of economic decentralization policies in a centralized party-state. We highlight the crucial role of intra-elite conflicts, particularly those between the authoritarian ruler and the increasingly powerful ruling elite who wield control over the state and party apparatus, in disrupting the institutional status quo and driving policy shifts. We establish a linkage between the elite composition of ruling parties and decentralization policies, thereby enhancing our understanding of policy-making dynamics in one-party regimes. We demonstrate that political shocks such as the Cultural Revolution, in part triggered by intra-elite conflicts in the state, can dramatically alter the composition of the ruling elite and reorient elite policy preferences, thus sustaining a particular policy direction such as economic decentralization in a relatively long period. Our findings also resonate with the second-generation fiscal federalism literature that examines political institutions with an emphasis on political parties (e.g., Filippov, Ordeshook, and Shvetsova, 2004; Garman, Haggard, and Willis, 2001; Riker, 1964; Weingast, 2009). Finally, a booming literature on authoritarianism provides insights into the function of authoritarian institutions in maintaining elite cohesion, but pays insufficient attention to the genesis of institutions (Pepinsky, 2014). In the context of market-preserving federalism in China, we offer a novel and consistent account of its origin, persistence, and retreat, thereby contributing to the discussion on the political origins of authoritarian institutions.

2 The Political Economy of Economic Decentralization

2.1 Economic Decentralization and China's Economic Miracle

The economic ascent of China in the past four decades has been truly astonishing and puzzling. Most impressively, China has transformed itself from a poor and isolated economy into a major global economic powerhouse, lifting nearly 800 million people out of poverty through a remarkable increase in GDP per capita from a meager US$156 in 1978 to US$10,409 in 2020.[1] Notably, the economic development of China has also challenged conventional wisdom that formal institutions, such as a credible constitution, are indispensable for safeguarding property rights and boosting economic growth (e.g., Acemoglu and Robinson, 2012; North, 1981). Although China's unorthodox economic reform did incorporate market forces, it diverged from the traditional Washington Consensus policies that were generally seen as necessary for economic success (Ang, 2016; Lin, 2011; Rodrik, 2006). While China's economic reform approach has not been without its challenges, it has nevertheless enabled China to achieve rapid economic growth, representing an intriguing alternative to the prevailing economic doctrine.

The literature on Chinese-style market-preserving federalism offers valuable insights into the origins of China's economic rise (Montinola, Qian, and Weingast, 1995; Qian, 2000; Qian and Roland, 1998; Qian and Weingast, 1997). Within this theoretical framework, "state predation" is recognized as the primary threat to property rights (North, 1990). As such, institutions must credibly limit the sovereign's political discretion to preserve markets. This theory posits that a set of institutional arrangements, particularly economic decentralization – delegating fiscal and regulatory authorities from the central government to subnational and local governments – can curb the interventionist role of the central government and thereby establish the political foundations for well-functioning markets.

As authority and resources are devolved away from the central government to local governments, local governments have incentives and de facto power to coordinate in resisting encroachment by the central government (Qian and Weingast, 1997). Fiscal decentralization also allows local and provincial governments to retain a large portion of marginal revenues, thus motivating subnational and local government officials to expand the tax base by promoting economic development (Montinola, Qian, and Weingast, 1995). Moreover, economic decentralization fosters jurisdictional competition

---

[1] Data source: the World Development Indicators Database (https://databank.worldbank.org/source/world-development-indicators).

among subnational or local governments, which in turn disciplines lower-level government officials and propels them to provide a hospitable policy environment for factors of production, including foreign capital (Montinola, Qian, and Weingast, 1995). Furthermore, Chinese-style federalism affords local governments considerable policy autonomy, nurturing favorable conditions for local policy experimentation. This policy experimentation – characterized by "innovation through implementation first, and then, later, the drafting of universal laws and regulations" – is a crucial component of China's successful reform (Heilmann, 2018, p. 78). As Montinola, Qian, and Weingast (1995, p. 78) note, "Experimentation, learning, and adaptation all follow from the inception of local political freedom over the economy."

Closely related, economic decentralization also gives rise to "local corporatism," wherein local governments are incentivized to spur economic growth by coordinating economic activities within their territories like diversified corporations with officials functioning as a board of directors (Oi, 1992). As fiscal reforms delineate ownership and impose harder budgetary constraints, local governments manage public industry as a diversified and market-oriented firm, with clearer incentives and greater ability to monitor public enterprises and enforce their interests as owners (Walder, 1995).

Empirically, scholars have documented that fiscal decentralization is associated with improved economic development. For example, Lin and Liu (2000) use provincial-level data from 1970 to 1993 to demonstrate that fiscal decentralization, as measured by marginal share rates, has a positive impact on economic growth. Similarly, Jin, Qian, and Weingast (2005) analyze provincial-level data from 1982 to 1992 and find evidence that the fiscal incentives of provincial governments prior to the tax-sharing reform facilitates market development.

The literature on Chinese-style federalism assumes that local government officials engage in competition for factors of production, with the objective of maximizing local government revenues. However, the competition among local governments, in the context of economic decentralization, may not necessarily lead to desirable outcomes (Cai and Treisman, 2004; Shleifer, 1997; Treisman, 1999). Economic decentralization can result in local protectionism and market fragmentation as local governments prioritize their own interests (Poncet, 2005; Young, 2000). The extensive involvement of local governments in economic development can also foster corruption and rent-seeking (Ang, 2020; Wedeman, 2012). Moreover, this theoretical framework rests on the assumption that the central government is inclined to intervene in the economy, and that decentralization to the local level would, to some extent, curb the central government's "grabbing hands," thereby facilitating economic growth. Yet it remains unclear how local governments can be powerful enough to constrain the central government's intervention. Consider, for example, that in the early 1990s, the central government removed recalcitrant provincial leaders from their posts, and ultimately established a more centralized tax-sharing system in 1994 (Cai and Treisman, 2006).

From a comparative perspective, fiscal decentralization in many countries failed to deliver robust economic growth (e.g., Davoodi and Zou, 1998; Thornton, 2007; Wibbels, 2000; Woller and Phillips, 1998). In contrast to China, Russia's economic decentralization in the 1990s was a salient failed case in terms of economic performance. One plausible explanation for this difference lies in the organizational structures of the former Soviet Union and China: the Soviet Union had a unitary-form (U-form) economy organized around specialized ministries, whereas China's economy had a multidivisional form (M-form) structure based on self-sufficient regions (Qian and Xu, 1993).[2] More importantly, the M-form structure promotes yardstick competition among regions more effectively (Maskin, Qian, and Xu, 2000) and has flexibility in experimentation and innovation (Qian, Roland, and Xu, 2006). In China, centralized political control is critical for the benefits of decentralization to materialize under yardstick competition, as the central government is able to appoint, dismiss, reward, or punish local governors, and those whose regions perform well can be promoted to the national government in Beijing (Blanchard and Shleifer, 2001).

The literature on "promotion tournaments" further delves into the microfoundations of China's economic growth by focusing on the *political* incentives of local government officials to pursue promotion, rather than the economic incentives of local governments to maximize fiscal revenues. According to this framework, the central government exerts personnel control over local officials and links performance evaluations to economic targets, thereby incentivizing the latter to boost economic growth within their jurisdictions to enhance their chances of promotion. In China, the CCP, specifically the Organization Department, wields personnel power and determines the career trajectories of local officials (Huang, 1999; Landry, 2008). Personnel control enables higher-level officials to monitor and ensure policy compliance (Edin, 2003). The "one-level-down management" system, established in 1984, stipulates that officials at each level control the appointment, promotion, dismissal, and transfer of officials one step down the administrative hierarchy (Landry, 2008).

---

[2] In the literature on organization theory, the U-form organizational structure represents a company managed as a single unit along functional lines, such as marketing and finance, with decision-making authority concentrated at the top, while the M-form structure involves a company divided into semi-autonomous units, with each division operating relatively independently (Chandler, 1962; Williamson, 1975).

During the reform era, higher levels of government have employed economic indicators, such as GDP growth rates or fiscal revenues, to assess the performance of lower-level officials and determine promotions. As promotions are tied to local economic development, to excel in the competitive promotion tournament, local officials must prioritize economic growth and outperform potential competitors in advancing the economic development of their governing jurisdictions. Empirical studies have consistently demonstrated a positive correlation between economic performance in governing jurisdictions and the promotion likelihood of subnational or local government officials (e.g., Bo, 1996; Choi, 2012; Landry, Lü, and Duan, 2018; Li and Zhou, 2005; Li et al., 2019; Whiting, 2000).[3]

Xu (2011) characterizes the fundamental institutional arrangements underpinning China's economic growth as a "regionally decentralized authoritarian system," with economic decentralization and political centralization as its defining features. In the course of China's economic growth, the central government has confronted the need to delegate economic authority to subnational and local governments, while still maintaining a certain level of political authority. The challenge, therefore, lies in striking a balance between asserting central control and decentralizing economic authority. Although central authority is indispensable in a decentralized system, it can also have negative consequences if it becomes too powerful. In the absence of a robust constitutional framework to ensure the enforcement of decentralization, the central government has every incentive and the ability to withdraw devolved economic power at any time, which renders decentralization itself often unsustainable (Cai and Treisman, 2006).

In summary, the extensive literature on Chinese federalism provides ample theoretical insights into and evidence concerning the linkages between economic decentralization and China's stunning economic performance in the reform era. However, it largely leaves unanswered the questions of how economic decentralization materialized in the first place and why fiscal and economic decentralization was sustained for a relatively long period despite the weak constitutional framework and the tight top-down control of the ruling CCP.

---

[3] For critiques of this strand of literature, please see Su et al. (2012) and Su, Tao, and Yang (2018). Shih, Adolph, and Liu (2012) provide evidence that factional ties with top leaders, rather than economic performance, constitute a crucial factor in the career advancement of political leaders. Jia, Kudamatsu, and Seim (2015) demonstrate that a complementary relationship exists between political connections and economic performance, suggesting that politically connected leaders are more likely to get promoted when they exhibit robust economic performance.

2.2 Political Foundations of Fiscal Decentralization

The literature on Chinese-style federalism is rooted in two theoretical traditions of fiscal federalism. The first tradition is welfare economics, which assumes that public officials are benevolent social planners acting to maximize social welfare (for a review, see Oates, 1999). From this perspective, decentralized federalism can align the incentives of local governments with citizens' preferences, as local governments often have better information on local conditions and are more responsive to citizens than the national government (e.g., Oates, 1972). Intergovernmental competition for capital and labor also helps reveal citizens' preferences and sort them into communities with preferred tax rates and public goods levels, ultimately prompting local governments to provide optimal public goods (Tiebout, 1956). The second tradition stems from the public choice school, assuming that politicians and bureaucrats are motivated by self-interest. Decentralization spurs jurisdictional competition and enables capital and labor to "vote with their feet," curbing the predatory tendencies of governments and constraining officials' abuse of power (e.g., Brennan and Buchanan, 1980; Buchanan, 1995; Weingast, 1995). In short, fiscal federalism can boost social welfare by improving information and promoting competition.

The classical theory of fiscal federalism is grounded in the context of a constitutional democracy, wherein the constitution delineates the boundaries between central and local authorities. In a decentralized setting, the central or federal government would encounter significant resistance in attempting to reclaim devolved powers due to the considerable costs associated with amending the constitutional system. As such, the stability of the decentralized system is an underlying assumption that is taken as given. Closely related, in much of the literature on fiscal federalism, federalism is realized through proper institutional design, which, once implemented, is assumed to be difficult to change (Bednar, 2003; Oates, 1999). In this vein, one crucial condition of Chinese-style federalism is that "the allocation of authority and responsibility has an institutionalized degree of durability" (Montinola, Qian, and Weingast, 1995, p. 55). Put another way, the demarcated powers between the national and subnational governments cannot be unilaterally changed by the national government. Overall, the classical approaches in economics "have assumed away problems of politics, incentives, and stability and have focused instead on the rather abstract efficiency and accountability" (Rodden, 2006, p. 18).

Inspired by the debates between Alexander Hamilton and Thomas Jefferson in the *Federalist Papers*, scholars in the field of political science have long recognized a fundamental tension inherent in establishing a well-functioning federal system, which revolves around a challenge of institutional design, specifically how to create a central government that is both strong and limited. The objective is to form a central government that is strong enough to effectively provide collective goods while simultaneously remaining sufficiently restrained to maintain local autonomy.

Perhaps more importantly, however, the realization of federalism is much more than a problem of institutional design, even in established democracies. In his seminal book *Federalism: Origins, Operation, Significance*, Riker (1964) notes that a well-functioning federalism requires a set of political institutions, especially political parties. Riker (1964, p. 51) posits that federalism is an outcome of institutional bargaining among politicians and "the structure of the system of political parties is what encourages or discourages the maintenance of the federal bargaining." In the case of the United States, decentralized parties can help limit encroachments from the national government: "The decentralization of the two-party system is sufficient to prevent national leaders (e.g., Presidents) from controlling their partisans by either organizational or ideological devices. As such, this decentralized party system is the main protector of the integrity of states in our federalism" (Riker, 1964, p. 101). Equally important, Riker's earlier work in the late 1950s suggests that federal–state partisan "disharmony," where the federal opposition party controls the states, correlates with lower levels of intergovernmental cooperation (Riker and Schaps, 1957). The implication is that national political parties can forge links between national and subnational politicians, thereby motivating subnational politicians to prioritize national collective goods and reduce negative externalities (Rodden, 2006).

Building on Riker's (1964) work, scholars have investigated the relationship between party systems and federalism. Integrated party systems contribute to the sustainability of federal systems by institutionalizing elite competition. Integrated party systems facilitate cooperation across government levels through promoting mutual dependence between politicians at different levels while granting them sufficient autonomy. In an integrated party system, national and local politicians depend on each other for reelection; the party's success at the national level bolsters local candidates' election prospects, while local organizations lend their support to the national party (Filippov, Ordeshook, and Shvetsova, 2004). Meanwhile, local branches and candidates retain enough autonomy to run their own campaigns tailored to their constituencies. Thus, integrated parties provide a crucial institutional mechanism for preserving federal systems.

The configuration of party systems offers a valuable perspective for understanding economic decentralization. Garman, Haggard, and Willis (2001, p. 207) have developed a theoretical framework to establish a linkage between political parties' control and accountability patterns and levels of fiscal decentralization: "if parties are more centralised, any bargaining over intergovernmental fiscal relations will favour the centre and the fiscal structure of the state will be more centralised. Conversely, if party control is less centralised, the state's fiscal structure will also tend to be more decentralised, other things being equal."[4]

By examining the party systems in place, we can gain insight into the distribution of power and decision-making processes, and how they affect economic performance in a federal system. Strong national parties help align the political incentives of local politicians with national goals by providing political support for local candidates during elections or promoting local politicians to national-level politics. Meanwhile, local elections hold local politicians accountable to their constituencies. Strong political parties can discipline co-partisans at subnational or local levels of government and provide incentives for them to internalize externalities, leading to better macroeconomic management outcomes, such as lower deficits and inflation (Rodden and Wibbels, 2002; Wibbels, 2001). In the case of Argentina, when provincial governors belong to the same party as the president, the president's party can induce the governors to have fiscal discipline (Jones, Sanguinetti, and Tommasi, 2000). More generally, a cross-national analysis of seventy-five developing and transition countries during 1975–2000 presents evidence that strong national political parties are associated with better outcomes of fiscal decentralization, such as economic growth, public goods provision, and government quality (Enikolopov and Zhuravskaya, 2007).

The institutional approach to understanding federalism has its limitations, as institutions are incomplete contracts (e.g., Tirole, 1999), and their rules and procedures are subject to various and sometimes contradictory interpretations (e.g., Mahoney and Thelen, 2009). Institutions can be epiphenomenal, reflecting deeper political, social, and economic relations and are often driven by social conflicts among actors seeking to protect their interests (Knight, 1992; Pepinsky, 2014; Shepsle, 2006). As a result, the beliefs, preferences, and networks of the individuals who run these institutions become more critical than the institutional rules themselves. The underlying distribution of de facto power, which can be understood as "informal constraints," such as the power configurations of actors, networks, and coalitions among political elites, plays a crucial role in shaping political and economic outcomes (Jiang, Xi, and Xie, 2024).

---

[4] It is worth noting that the (de)centralization of the party systems may be shaped by the levels of fiscal (de)centralization (Chibber and Kollman, 2004; Harbers, 2010).

As such, both the structure of party systems and fiscal (de)centralization could be endogenous to elite power dynamics. In the case of Mexico, for example, both party centralization and fiscal centralization resulted from elite bargaining and compromises (Diaz-Cayeros, 2006). Mexican politicians centralized political authority in the middle of the twentieth century through a regional compromise that involved creating a hegemonic political party, the Partido Revolucionario Institucional (PRI). The PRI's control of the electoral process and local political careers allowed it to gain influence over local politicians, enabling the central government to centralize revenue collection, which required national politicians to protect regional politicians from challengers and electoral threats in exchange for financial resources.

Ultimately, as Riker (1975, p. 141) points out, the essence of federalism lies in "the political bargain that creates it," as well as "the distribution of power in political parties which shapes the federal structure in its maturity." Therefore, a balance of power among national and local elites in a party system helps sustain federal systems: The dominance of national elites in party systems may alter institutions to weaken local government powers; a party system dominated by local elites, on the other hand, is more likely to compel national elites to accept subnational government common pool behavior (Weingast, 2009).

Overall, much of the literature on federalism assumes a democratic setting with a credible constitution and pays relatively less attention to the other problem identified by (Riker, 1964), that is, the central authority's predatory behavior to make claims on local revenue or to intervene in local decision making in ways that undermine federalist arrangements (Bednar, Eskridge, and Ferejohn, 2001; Garman, Haggard, and Willis, 2001). In the absence of credible constitutions or institutionalized electoral and party systems, the center may roll back regional privileges, rendering federal concessions temporary (Bahry, 2005). This precarious dynamic is especially pronounced in weak democracies and authoritarian regimes, where political institutions lack perpetuity and rules can be rewritten by leaders on a whim, allowing leaders to renege on the federalist arrangements at a relatively low cost (Weingast, 2014).

2.3 Party-State Building, Elite Composition, and Economic Policies

As previously discussed, the distribution of power within the party system is crucial for understanding the sustainability of federalism. To gain a deep understanding of how political power is distributed under authoritarian regimes and the conditions under which economic decentralization can be sustained, it is essential to explore the origins and evolution of elite power configurations.

In the case of mainland China, we examine the formation of the party-state and the ruling party's elite composition over time to explain why mainland China's economic decentralization took place and was sustained for a relatively long period of time. We aim to understand the dynamics of political clout between central and local elites, as well as its impact on economic decentralization.

After decades of violent revolutions and warfare, the CCP established a powerful and centralized party-state in mainland China in the mid twentieth century. Revolutions are characterized by "rapid and basic transformations of a society's state and class structures" and often fundamentally reshape state–society relations (Skocpol, 1979, p. 4). Sustained political and class struggles force revolutionaries to build coercive capacity to cope with internal and external threats (Gurr, 1988; Skocpol, 1988). As a result, most revolutions produce a powerful coercive state apparatus and destroy alternative power centers (Levitsky and Way, 2022).

The Chinese communist revolution illustrates these dynamics. In 1927, the alliance between the Kuomintang (KMT) and the CCP collapsed. To eradicate the CCP, the KMT launched encirclement campaigns against CCP base areas in the 1930s. The CCP armies abandoned their base in Jiangxi province and undertook the Long March to Shaanxi province. Only about 30,000 troops remained when they arrived in Yan'an, Shaanxi, losing nearly 90 percent during the Long March (Jiang, 2006). The Long March established Mao Zedong as the CCP's de facto leader and reinforced the Party's elite cohesion. Although the Long March "had started amid suspicion, jealousy, intrigue, and fears, with Mao on the sidelines," it ended with "hard confidence" in the Party leadership and the revolution (Salisbury, 1985, p. 325). The Long March survivors gained prestige in the CCP and served as its backbone until the early 1990s.

The Yan'an Rectification Campaign of 1942–43 further strengthened Party discipline and unity around Mao (Walder, 2015, chapter 2). This campaign was characterized by a blend of "theoretical indoctrination and brute intimidation" (Gao, 2018, p. 453). Initially targeting intellectuals, it gradually evolved into an extensive purge of suspected traitors and spies within the Party. The cadre investigation, which involved screening the files of cadres and Party members, employed torture, sleep and food deprivation, and mock executions to extract confessions. Approximately 15,000 "secret agents" were purged, detained, censored, and subjected to mental and physical abuse, with some even executed (Gao, 2018, p. 648). The pervasive fear instilled by the campaign made it treasonous to disagree with Party policies. As a result, "a fear of implication in traitorous activities" induced "conformity" to the Party and its policies (Seybolt, 1986).

The Sino-Japanese War compelled the KMT to abandon its stronghold in the prosperous lower-Yangtze region and relocate to Chongqing, a city in the mountainous southwest of China. The CCP seized the opportunity presented by the Sino-Japanese War to expand its forces into northern and northwestern China, especially mountainous and remote areas behind Japanese lines. By the end of the Sino-Japanese War, the CCP had established nineteen base areas with more than one million troops, paving the way for defeating the KMT in the ensuing Civil War. The Civil War forced the CCP to build a powerful state and military apparatus, laying the foundations for "a vast, militarized bureaucracy that excelled at extracting sacrifice from subject populations and party cadres alike" (Walder, 2015, p. 39).

Perhaps more importantly, the prolonged revolution also undermined and dismantled alternative centers of power (Levitsky and Way, 2022). During the Civil War, the CCP implemented radical land reforms in North China between 1946 and 1947, which in effect destroyed the wealth and power of traditional rural elites (e.g., Hinton, 1966; Pepper, 1999; Zhi, 2008). The struggle meetings *(pidou hui)* during the land reforms often "ended in the summary execution of landlords and the seizure and division of their property" (Walder, 2015, p. 46). In the early 1950s, another wave of land reform wiped out nearly one million landlords and their family members (e.g., Dikötter, 2013). Meanwhile, other political campaigns, such as the Campaign to Suppress Counterrevolutionaries, the Three-Anti Campaign, and the Five-Anti Campaign, arrested and executed millions of former KMT officials, capitalists, bandits, local strongmen, religious sect leaders, and secret society members (e.g., Strauss, 2006; Yang, 2008).

By the end of 1956, the communist state had nearly completed the agricultural collectivization and nationalization of industries and financial institutions so that private property was virtually eradicated. As a result, the gentry class were replaced by "young peasant activists drawn from the poor peasantry" and the CCP authorities extended their reach to the village level (Meisner, 1999, p. 100). In urban areas, the CCP eradicated propertied old elites and expanded its power into communities, workplaces, and families (e.g., Walder, 1986). Ultimately, a totalitarian state marked by the dominance of a single monolithic Party and the party-state's deep penetration of society was established in China (Barnett, 1960; Walker, 1955).

The hallmark of China's political system is the fusion of party and state, namely the party-state. As Shirk (1993, p. 58) notes, "the Communist Party selects all government officials; almost all government officials and all top officials are themselves party members; and in each government agency, party members are organized at the higher administrative level." In effect, the

Chinese state apparatus falls under the political domination of the CCP. The CCP exercises control through the *nomenklatura* system, encompassing lists of leading positions subject to Party committee appointments, reserve cadre lists, and institutions/processes for personnel changes (Burns, 1987). This hierarchical system of Party committees, extending downward from the Central Committee, runs parallel to the multilayered bureaucracy. The Central Committee represents the power elite in the Chinese political system. Although not all powerful figures are present in the Central Committee at any particular moment, the CCP power elite can be most comprehensively identified in the Central Committee (Shih, Shan, and Liu, 2010a). Assuming that the composition of the Central Committee could largely reflect the power distribution within the elite political equilibrium (Shih, Shan, and Liu, 2010b), it clearly points to a remarkably high level of political centralization in the Chinese state during the 1950s. This was particularly evident during the Eighth Party Congress in 1956, where approximately 80 percent of the Central Committee members held positions in the central government or the central Party apparatus in Beijing. Considering the entrenched interest of the elites in the central state apparatus to maintain the status quo, it becomes even more puzzling why a politically centralized state would eventually opt to decentralize its economic resources and authority to subnational and local governments.

To unravel this puzzle, we offer a novel perspective that highlights the elite conflicts within the state, particularly between the authoritarian ruler and the ruling elites at the upper echelons of the regime.[5] The overarching goal of authoritarian rulers is to retain their grip on power for political survival (e.g., Bueno de Mesquita et al., 2003; Tullock, 1987; Wintrobe, 2000). Authoritarian rulers, for various reasons, find it necessary to delegate power to or engage in power-sharing with other ruling elites (e.g., Meng, Paine, and Powell, 2023). The ruling elites who wield control over the state apparatus are not merely "agents" carrying out the will of the principal – the ruler. Rather, certain powerful elites could potentially pose a formidable threat to the ruler. As Tullock (1987, p. 28) insightfully put it, "in a very real sense a dictator lives in a state of nature. He is not the owner of important assets in a well-run state. There is no overwhelmingly powerful state which can protect him. What he needs to be protected from are parts of the state." Even worse, a centralized and relatively institutionalized state apparatus allows powerful elites to cultivate

---

[5] An emerging body of literature on intra-elite conflict and state capacity mostly concerns either the conflict between agricultural elites and capitalist elites (Beramendi, Dincecco, and Rogers, 2019; Mares and Queralt, 2015) or between state actors and economic elites (Garfias, 2018, 2019). Our theoretical framework focuses on intra-elite conflict within the state (for a recent study, see Garfias and Sellars, 2021).

their support base, amass their de facto power, and organize and coordinate actions effectively. As the state machinery or bureaucracy attains a certain level of autonomy – referring to their ability to exercise discretionary authority in implementing policies set by political principals as well as formulating policies aligned with their own preferences (Bersch and Fukuyama, 2023) – the governing elites commanding the state machinery may advance their own agenda, disregarding policies favored by the authoritarian ruler. As a result, maintaining political control over the state machinery becomes a paramount concern for authoritarian rulers.

Over the course of history, political leaders have sought to maintain a dedicate balance between bureaucratic autonomy and political control (Andersen and Møller, 2019). For instance, the Ottomans maintained control through a system of military slavery, employing eunuchs and Christian youths as governors and administrators, who were raised as Turkish-speaking Muslims to serve the sultan (Fukuyama, 2011, chapter 13). In imperial China, the emperor's power was exercised through the bureaucratic machinery. The top-down delegation process and the bureaucracy's internal routines gave rise to tensions with the emperor's authority (Zhou, 2022, p. 39). The emperor constantly battled against a routinized and bloated bureaucracy, occasionally turning to political campaigns to disrupt routine and subject officials to the emperor's autocratic control (e.g., Kuhn, 1990). To be sure, political leaders can strengthen their political control over the bureaucracy through performance management tactics like monitoring, rewarding, and punishing (e.g., Finan, Olken, and Pande, 2017; McCubbins, Noll, and Weingast, 1987), as well as through regular personnel management practices such as appointment, transfer, and removal (Iyer and Mani, 2012; Toral, 2023).

However, it is crucial to recognize that these conventional measures may not be effective in revolutionary regimes. The Chinese communist revolution, characterized by protracted warfare, spawned a substantial cohort of revolutionary veterans. These veterans, endowed with extensive political networks throughout the Party, state, and military apparatuses, possessed formidable capacities for collective action, thereby presenting existential threats to the authoritarian ruler's grip on power. Conventional personnel control measures often fall short in curbing the expansion of political networks and the accumulation of de facto power by such powerful elites. Put differently, it remains difficult for an authoritarian ruler to reduce the odds of potential challenge from powerful political elites through the mechanisms of personnel control. Frequent job rotations may prevent political elites from establishing a stronghold within their assigned role. However, for revolutionary veterans, they had already developed extensive political networks that spanned various state institutions.

Even if a leader was ousted or purged, his/her successor probably would possess a comparably extensive political network due to the large pool of revolutionary veterans.

In an effort to mitigate threats from influential elites, authoritarian rulers could opt to decentralize resources from the central government to local entities. This strategy helps prevent the concentration of power among political elites within central Party and state institutions by limiting their control over valuable resources. The threats posed by powerful local leaders are less of a concern in a hierarchical one-party authoritarian regime. Without the collaboration of senior officials in the central bureaucracy, local leaders are unlikely to pose a considerable challenge to the ruler. More crucially, authoritarian rulers can strategically manipulate the composition or the size of the ruling coalition, that is, the selectorate (Bueno de Mesquita et al., 2003). They can elevate more local leaders into the ruling coalition as a counterbalance to the influence of powerful elites in the central Party and state institutions. In essence, they can form a ruling coalition with relatively weak figures, such as those with narrow political networks or those lacking experience in national-level politics (Shih, 2022).[6]

The analysis thus far leads to several observable implications. First, the preferences of authoritarian rulers may not align with those of influential elites in the central bureaucracy when it comes to economic policies. While the latter may favor centralization policies that allow them to amass power, the former may curb such efforts and lean toward decentralization policies (Fewsmith, 2016; Shih, 2008). Second, authoritarian rulers might strive to reshuffle the ruling coalition by diminishing the representation of powerful central elites, thereby neutralizing potential threats. Third, perhaps most importantly, the composition of the ruling coalition is closely associated with economic decentralization. When local leaders dominate the ruling coalition, economic decentralization is more likely to be sustained, as will be elaborated upon shortly.

Through the lens of the ruling coalition's elite composition, we present a novel perspective on China's economic decentralization. Our account begins with the pivotal role of nominally representative institutions, such as the CCP's Central Committee, in binding authoritarian rulers to a given set of policies by imposing costs for policy reversals. A substantial body of

---

[6] Following the same logic, in the Tang dynasty of imperial China, Empress Wu Zetian encountered pushback and resistance from the established elites upon assuming power. In response, she "diluted the existing powerholders by expanding the Keju pipeline to outsiders and newcomers" (Huang, 2023, p. 46). Prior to this change, the vast majority of Keju candidates were selected from elite aristocratic families.

theoretical literature on authoritarian regimes suggests that regimes with une-lected representative bodies comprising segments of the elite can credibly assure a certain payoff stream to the elite (Boix and Svolik, 2013; Gandhi, 2008; Gehlbach and Keefer, 2011; Magaloni, 2008; Svolik, 2012). Authori-tarian rulers establish these representative institutions to aggregate the heter-ogeneous preferences of their supporters, thereby reducing governance costs and providing credible signals of future streams of payoffs. As representative institutions like the Central Committee lower the transaction costs of staging a challenge or even a coup against the authoritarian ruler, they credibly com-mit the authoritarian ruler to the promised stream of payments to the elite (Boix and Svolik, 2013; Gehlbach and Keefer, 2012). These insights further reinforce the observation that authoritarian leaders, although not elected, still rely on a small selectorate to stay in power (Bueno de Mesquita et al., 2003; Shirk, 1993).

The selectorate theory underscores the mechanism of "reciprocal accounta-bility," which stems from Susan Shirk's insightful observation of the Chinese political system: "Government officials are both the agents and constituents of the party leaders; local officials are both the agents and constituents of the central leaders. Officials hold their positions at the pleasure of the party lead-ership, but party leaders hold their positions at the pleasure of the officials in the selectorate" (Shirk, 1993). In addition to the relative size of the win-ning coalition, the composition of the selectorate also warrants consideration (Gallagher and Hanson, 2015).

In this view of authoritarian regimes, authoritarian rulers would be wise to pursue policies favored by a winning coalition within the selectorate, partic-ularly if they govern through a representative institution such as the Central Committee; otherwise, they would encounter higher costs of staying in power. This links the composition of the selectorate to the policies likely to be pursued by the authoritarian rulers. While members of the selectorate share common preferences, such as more privileged benefits from the government, their varied institutional affiliations within the regime give rise to heterogeneous pref-erences. For example, provincial-level officials in less developed provinces prefer greater concentration of investment in provincial capitals, compared to more affluent provinces, because they saw such concentration of investment as the fastest way of catching up (Jaros, 2019). Thus, refashioning the composi-tion of the selectorate would alter the policy preferences of the authoritarian ruler, who seeks to minimize the cost of staying in power, as long as the policy change does not endanger any other core interest of the authoritarian ruler.

In China, both exogenous shocks and endogenous processes brought about a change in the composition of the ruling elite, which in turn reoriented the

Table 1 Deductive implications of our theory

	Local domination	Absence of local domination
Economic decentralization	Success (1970–1994)	Failure (1958–1961)
Economic centralization	Failure (1980s)	Success (1961–1966; 1994–)

incentives of the top leadership toward either pursuing decentralization policies or advocating for centralization policies. To be sure, the composition of the selectorate likely evolves endogenously at the margins, shaped by various policy outcomes. Nevertheless, the composition of the selectorate in one-party regimes tends to exhibit stickiness due to the high transaction costs associated with major leadership reshuffling, thus rendering it an exogenous variable in the short and medium term (Nathan, 1973; Pepinsky, 2009). In rare instances, the benefits of a major reshuffling outweigh the costs, instigating exogenous political shocks that drastically reshape the composition of the selectorate. These shocks, in turn, alter the incentives for authoritarian rulers to pursue one policy over another. Even though institutions and norms remain largely unchanged, shifting incentives for rulers can make de facto federalism a reality even in an authoritarian regime (Bednar, Eskridge, and Ferejohn, 2001).

In the context of mainland China, we posit that the dominance of local officials within the CCP's Central Committee was a *necessary* condition for sustained economic decentralization, although a top-down command or another form of shock also set it into motion. This theoretical argument gives rise to four deductive implications, illustrated in Table 1: (1) when local officials dominate the selectorate, economic decentralization is implemented and persists (the top-left cell); (2) when local officials do not dominate the selectorate, economic decentralization is either not implemented or fails to persist (the top-right cell); (3) when local officials dominate, economic centralization fails (the bottom-left cell); and (4) when local officials do not dominate, economic centralization succeeds (the bottom-right cell).

This Element will focus on the most powerful exogenous shock since 1949, which was the Cultural Revolution (1966–1976). The Cultural Revolution drastically reshaped the composition of the selectorate by purging most of the senior central officials from their government and party positions. Mao's power plays were not motivated by economic goals but gave rise to a Central Committee dominated by local officials at the 1969 Ninth Party Congress and the

1973 Tenth Party Congress. Our data on Central Committee composition reveal that the dominance of local officials established at the outset of the Cultural Revolution persisted through subsequent Party congresses owing to relatively lower turnovers in later congresses. Upon ascending to power in 1978, Deng Xiaoping sensibly perpetuated decentralization policies to appease the dominant constituency in the political elite at that time. In contrast, the decentralization during the Great Leap Forward (1958–1962) was not accompanied by elite reshuffling, which resulted in its reversal shortly thereafter. The top leadership's strong preference for decentralization did not change until the 1990s, following a decade of central bureaucracy rebuilding. Throughout these periods, the composition of the CCP elite in the Central Committee, rather than institutional changes, provided a vital foundation for top leaders to pursue either centralization or decentralization policies.

To demonstrate the generalizability of our findings, we examine a shadow case – Taiwan under the Kuomintang (KMT)'s authoritarian rule – and illustrate the presence of similar patterns that link the composition of the party elite with policy orientation. The case of Taiwan suggests that Taiwan's economic liberalization, especially the transition from an import substitution industrialization policy to an export-led growth strategy in the late 1950s, was accompanied by a marked decline in the political clout of the Executive Yuan representatives (central technocrats) within the KMT's Central Committee. It is important to emphasize that Taiwan's case in our study is not directly compared in a cross-case analysis. Instead, our research design gains inferential leverage through process tracing within-case studies (e.g., Collier, 2011; Mahoney, 2012).

Our analysis proceeds in chronological order, systematically tracing the decision-making process surrounding each pivotal moment in history. To begin with, we examine the elite's conflicts over economic policies between Mao and other political leaders, particularly those in the State Council. Mao championed economic decentralization and the mobilization of local initiatives, whereas the State Council planners remained committed to a practical state plan. As Mao's policy stances prevailed, the Great Leap Forward (1958–1961) saw the first wave of economic decentralization in China. Subsequently, we delve into the reversal of decentralization policies following the Great Leap Forward, attributable to the dominant clout wielded by central officials within the Central Committee (top right cell of Table 1). The Cultural Revolution, a sweeping purge of the party initiated by Mao's growing suspicions toward his colleagues, fundamentally reshaped the elite composition of the Central Committee, thereby rendering economic decentralization policies sustainable (top left cell of Table 1). As a substantial portion of the followers belonging to these purged factions, as well as other capitalist elements targeted by

Mao, were central officials, a large number of high-level central bureaucrats were removed from the upper echelons of the Party. Consequently, the central bureaucrats became a relatively weakened political force for the subsequent two decades. After this significant reorientation of elite power dynamic, it made good political sense for Mao to pursue decentralization regardless of his policy preference.

As Deng assumed power in the late 1970s, the provincial dominance in the Central Committee was an established fact, one that Deng could not have immediately altered without incurring considerable costs. A much less costly and more sensible strategy was to give major concessions to provincial interests in order to win local support for his political struggle against his competitors. Among other things, such concessions took the form of continued fiscal and enterprise decentralization. The policy outcomes observed throughout the 1980s aligned with the implications outlined in the left-bottom cell of Table 1.

Throughout the 1980s, both endogenous evolution and exogenous pressure gradually elevated the representation of central technocrats in the Central Committee. Endogenously, decentralization policies engendered a growing array of economic challenges that necessitated a larger and more competent central state to address (Shih, 2008; Wedeman, 2003). At the same time, the top leaders' desire to diminish the military's role in elite politics and the passing of the veteran revolutionary generation led to a new generation of young, educated technocrats assuming leadership roles in an expanding number of central organs. Given that these positions entailed guaranteed admission into the Central Committee, the share of central officials in the Central Committee also rose steadily throughout the second half of the 1980s and the first half of the 1990s.

When the Tiananmen unrest and the collapse of the Soviet Union shocked the top leadership into action, pursuing centralization policies was no longer politically difficult. As the leadership set forth to implement centralization policies such as fiscal centralization and "grasping the big and letting go of the small" (*zhua da fang xiao*) in the mid-1990s, they secured the support of a powerful coalition comprising central technocrats and Party officials within the Central Committee. This scenario fits neatly into the bottom right cell of Table 1.

A crucial element of our argument is that large-scale elite reshuffling in the CCP was rare after the founding of the People's Republic of China. Figure 1 displays the incumbency ratio of the Central Committee (CC). At the 1956 Eighth Party Congress, nearly 60 percent of full CC members had been full or alternate CC members at the Seventh Party Congress. Mao's Cultural Revolution radically reshuffled the elite such that by the 1969 Ninth Party Congress, only 30 percent of the full CC members had served in the previous CC as full

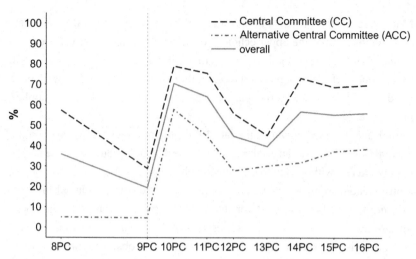

Figure 1 Overall, Central Committee (CC), and Alternate Central Committee (ACC) incumbency ratios: 8th–16th Party Congresses.

or alternate members.[7] No other leader in China, including Mao himself, was able to replicate such a degree of elite reshuffling. Throughout the remainder of the Cultural Revolution, the incumbency ratio of full CC members remained remarkably high, reaching nearly 80 percent. While the 13th Party Congress registered an overall incumbency ratio of less than 50 percent among full CC members due to the retirement policy, it was still 15 percent higher than the incumbency ratio at the Ninth Party Congress. During the 1990s, the incumbency ratio of full CC members settled around 70 percent, meaning that it took a decade, spanning two Party congresses, to witness a turnover in the majority of the Central Committee. Therefore, after the Cultural Revolution, the change in elite composition became a slow-moving, decade-long process that ensured the medium-term stability of the degree of decentralization.

The relatively high incumbency ratio and the sizable representation by central technocrats and SOE managers spanning from Hu Jintao's to Xi Jinping's periods (e.g., Brødsgaard, 2012) imply that policy centralization will continue as the predominant approach to economic management in the foreseeable future. As sustainable decentralization does not appear to be a viable route for reform, Chinese leaders will need to explore new avenues for fashioning reform coalitions and developing credible reform policies.

---

[7] Mao wielded substantial influence over the selection of CC members, allowing him to manipulate the elite composition of the CC of the Ninth Party Congress. Before the convening of the Ninth Party Congress, Zhou Enlai proposed a list of 115 CC members to Mao. However, Mao advocated for a more sizable CC, ultimately resulting in the inclusion of 170 full members and 109 alternates (MacFarquhar and Schoenhals, 2006, p. 292).

Alternative Explanations When considering alternative explanations, scholars typically focus on Mao's grand vision for communism or the dismantling of central planning capacities during the Cultural Revolution as reasons for the shift toward decentralization policies. Maskin, Qian, and Xu (2000), Qian, Roland, and Xu (2006), and Xu (2011) rightly note the Maoist legacy of decentralization, pointing out that China's economy, even under Mao's rule, operated on a geographical rather than a functional basis, setting it apart from the Soviet Union. Whiting (2000) also draws attention to the impact of the Maoist ideal of self-reliance on the regional variations in rural industrial development during the Maoist era. However, these accounts do not adequately explain the persistence of Maoist policies well into the 1980s, despite extensive reshuffling of top leadership.

Although it is widely acknowledged that the policy preferences of top leaders can have a profound influence on outcomes in authoritarian regimes (Jones and Olken, 2005; Treisman, 2015), we are not convinced it tells the whole story here. Even if Mao genuinely had preferred decentralization, we show clear evidence that many of the decentralization policies were rolled back after the end of the Great Leap Forward in 1961, suggesting that economic policies and institutions lacked stickiness (Lardy, 1975). The malleability of economic institutions further adds to the puzzle of economic decentralization in the Deng era. When Deng ascended to the top position in the CCP, he steered policies away from autarky and collective agriculture (Fewsmith, 2016; Shirk, 1993). Given Deng's clear wishes to distance himself from the excesses of the Cultural Revolution, it remains puzzling why he opted to follow Mao's footsteps and pursue decentralization.

To be sure, it is plausible that Deng, like Mao, held a strong preference for decentralization. However, upon examining the policies Deng pursued prior to the reform era, it becomes evident that he did not consistently champion decentralization. Like many other senior leaders, Deng supported Mao's radical decentralization policies during the Great Leap Forward, but he also contributed to the economic recovery in the aftermath of the Great Leap Forward, which witnessed a shift toward re-centralization (Donnithorne, 1980; MacFarquhar, 1983). Moreover, given Deng's enduring influence even after the Southern Tour, why did he allow fiscal centralization to occur in 1994?

Beyond the great man hypothesis, scholars also argue that the Cultural Revolution ravaged the central bureaucracy so that it no longer had the capacity to fully reinstate a centralized planned economy in China after 1976 (Shirk, 1993; Walder, 2016). Indeed, the State Planning Commission, the linchpin of the centralized planned economy, lost nearly 90 percent of its cadres by 1970 (Oksenberg and Tong, 1991). The Ministry of Finance was so disrupted by

Red Guard activities that it was occupied by the military between 1967 and 1975 (Xiang, 1999). However, the central bureaucracy had been on the mend since the Lin Biao Incident in 1971 (e.g., Swaine, 1986).[8] By the early 1980s, the State Planning Commission regained its leading role in making pivotal decisions concerning production, prices, and investment (Shih, 2008).

Finally, another perspective emphasizes the catastrophic aftermath of the Cultural Revolution. The ideological bankruptcy and economic devastation that ensued led the elite and the public alike to abandon the old communist doctrines and economic systems, turning instead to alternative ideologies and economic policies. As MacFarquhar and Schoenhals (2006, p. 459) point out, "In the succeeding quarter-century, Mao's worst revisionist nightmare has been realized, with only himself to blame...it was Mao's disastrous enactment of his utopian fantasies that freed Deng's mind from Communist orthodoxies." Similarly, Bernstein (2013, p. 43) posits that after the Cultural Revolution, "the elite and the population were exhausted, traumatized, and repelled by years of class struggle and factional and state violence. The public longed for stability and a better life. In short, the country was ready for something new." Moreover, in the aftermath of the Cultural Revolution, as stated by Hua Guofeng, the supreme leader of China at the time, the Chinese economy was "on the brink of collapse" (Field, 1986, p. 625), prompting an urgent need for economic development and the improvement of people's living standards. While these insights enhance our understanding of the demand-side factors driving China's economic reform, they do not offer a comprehensive explanation of the supply-side dynamics, including the political power configuration and elite decision making within the CCP leadership that facilitated decentralization.

Departing from previous explanations, our account explains the rise of decentralization policies in the early 1970s, the continuation of these policies through leadership changes in the late 1970s and into the 1980s, as well as the sudden reversal of decentralization policies in the early 1960s. Furthermore, our account predicts the re-emergence of fiscal and enterprise re-centralization in the 1990s, as well as the persistence of a centralized mode of economic policy into the foreseeable future.

3 Mainland

3.1 Data and Methods

While the existing literature focuses primarily on fiscal decentralization, we adopt a broader perspective to conceptualize economic decentralization.

---

[8] Following Premier Zhou Enlai's request in 1970 to reinstate major statistical report forms, the State Statistical Bureau effectively maintained specialized statistical reporting systems (Field, 1986).

According to (Xu, 2011), economic decentralization entails the delegation of governance authority over the national economy to subnational governments. In economically decentralized economies, regional entities, including provinces, municipalities, and counties, are relatively self-contained, with subnational governments assuming overall responsibility for initiating and coordinating reforms, delivering public services, and enacting and enforcing laws within their jurisdictions. In line with this, we conceptualize economic decentralization as the devolution of authority in the control and allocation of economic resources, such as fiscal revenues, investment funds, and state-owned enterprises (SOEs), from the central government to subnational and local governments. In this Element, we will focus on a set of indicators – including the ratio of local revenues to national revenues, the percentage of nonstate budgetary investment in capital construction in total capital construction investment, and the non-SOE share of industrial output – to keep track of the economic decentralization and centralization cycles.

Regarding our primary explanatory variable, ruling elite composition, we follow Shirk (1993) by assuming that the Central Committee (CC) comprises the bulk of the country's political elite and can be regarded as the selectorate in China. Full CC members typically hold pivotal positions in central ministries, Party organs, military institutions, local authorities, and they vote on crucial decisions at CC plenums. We leverage a quantitative database that includes every CC member and traces their entire career trajectories, to assemble time-series data on the annual percentage of central, provincial, and military officials among CC members from 1956 to 2006 (Shih, Shan, and Liu, 2010a).[9]

Our analysis centers on the proportion of CC members serving in central authorities such as central ministries and Party organs in comparison to those in local authorities. We employ three different definitions to identify central CC members. The first definition includes only those who served in a central Party or State Council organ during a specified time frame, typically a specific year. A broader second definition also accounts for CC members who held positions in the National People's Congress (NPC) Standing Committee, the Chinese People's Political Consultative Conference (CPPCC) National Committee, and the Supreme Court or Procuracy. As depicted in Figure 2, both definitions of central CC members exhibit similar trends. In Figure 3, we restrict the definition of central CC members to include only State Council and central State-Owned Enterprise (SOE) officials given their high stakes in maintaining central economic authorities (Shih, 2008). In addition, we define provincial CC members

---

[9] The Central Committee is usually elected in the autumn of the year. We consider the year of the Party congress as the starting point of a new term, as CC selection often takes place well in advance of the congress (Nathan and Gilley, 2002).

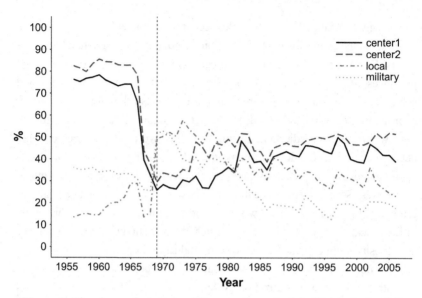

Figure 2 The share of central, military, and provincial officials in the CC.

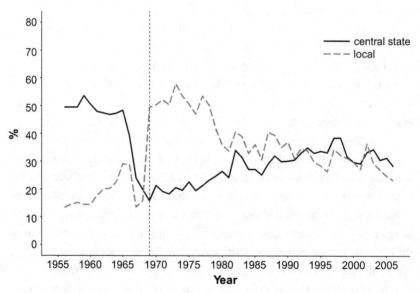

Figure 3 The share of central state and provincial officials in the CC.

as CC members who held party or government positions at the provincial or regional level in a given year. Finally, military CC members refer to those who served in the People's Liberation Army (PLA), including the Central Military Commission (CMC), PLA headquarters, and the military regions.

3.2 Prelude to the Great Leap Forward: Elite Conflicts at the Top Leadership

In the 1950s, Mao and the State Council planners, including Premier Zhou Enlai, the first-ranking Vice Premier Chen Yun, Vice Premier and Minister of Finance Li Xiannian, Vice Premier Deng Zihui in charge of agriculture, and Vice Premier and Chairman of the State Economic Commission Bo Yibo, disagreed and clashed over economic policies (e.g., MacFarquhar, 1974; Teiwes and Sun, 1999). The State Council planners held the view that economic development should be regulated to curb high targets, and that overall balance was essential. In contrast, Mao saw fast economic growth as crucial after the "socialist transformation" of production relations. These divergent perspectives on economic development highlighted a pronounced tension within the CCP's leadership, with Mao prioritizing speedy economic growth to achieve the desired socialist revolution, while the State Council planners sought to ensure a more cautious and balanced approach to economic development.[10]

In 1955, Mao advocated for a rapid rural collectivization as part of his broader campaign to accelerate socialist transformation in the countryside, whereas Deng Zihui, then the Vice Premier responsible for rural affairs, took a more cautious stance and was reluctant to embrace such a radical approach. At a meeting with provincial officials in July 1955, Mao focused on the collectivization of agriculture and conveyed his displeasure with State Council officials, particularly Deng Zihui: "In the countryside, the upsurge of a new socialist mass movement is approaching. Some comrades, however, are hobbling like a woman with bound feet and are always complaining that others are walking fast, walking fast" (Mao, 1977, p. 168).

In October 1955, during the Seventh Plenary Session of the Sixth Central Committee, the meeting resolution explicitly emphasized that "In light of the ever-growing enthusiasm for the rural cooperative movement, the Party's task is to lead the movement forward in a courageous and planned manner, instead of being hesitant or timid," while criticizing the Party's moderate leaders for

---

[10] During the early 1950s, Mao Zedong and other prominent political leaders, most notably Liu Shaoqi, held divergent views on how to approach the issue of urban capitalists, wealthy rural peasants, and labor unions (Lin, 2017, chapter 3). In December 1952, Bo Yibo, then the Vice Director of the Financial and Economic Commission of the State Council and Minister of Finance, put forward a new tax system that treated public and private enterprises equally. Mao criticized Bo heavily for "not reporting to the Party center in advance" and "putting capitalists above the Party center" (Bo, 1991, p. 235). Mao also expressed his dissatisfaction with Liu Shaoqi and Zhou Enlai to a select group of Party leaders. This discontent arguably played a role in the Gao-Rao affair, which took place between 1953 and 1955 and marked the first significant power struggle among Party elites since the establishment of the People's Republic of China in 1949 (Lin, 2017).

their "right-leaning opportunism" (*youqing jihui zhuyi*) and "lacking trust in the masses, being pessimistic about the Party center's cooperative policies and the leadership of local Party committees at all levels." [11]

In the summer of 1955, the State Council began to work on a fifteen-year plan for the national economy development and the outline of the Second Five-Year Plan. In October, upon reviewing the report drafted by the State Planning Commission, Mao expressed dissatisfaction with the planned pace of development. In December 1955, when writing the Preface to *Socialist Upsurge in China's Countryside (zhongguo nongcun de shehui zhuyi gaochao)*, Mao asserted that "the current problem is that many people believe they cannot accomplish certain tasks that could actually be achieved through effort. Therefore, it is absolutely necessary to continuously criticize the indeed existing "right-wing conservative ideologies" (*youqing baoshou zhuyi sixiang*) (Mao, 1977, p. 224). In 1956, the *People's Daily* published an editorial on New Year's Day that introduced the principle of "more, faster, better, and more economically" (*duo, kuai, hao, sheng*) for building socialism, which called for greater productivity, efficiency, quality, and cost-effectiveness in the pursuit of economic development.[12] This principle, in effect, galvanized a bold and adventurous thinking for economic development throughout the country.

In February 1956, Premier Zhou Enlai warned against the high targets in the industrialization plan:

> When ministries and departments set their plans, whether it is a 12-year long-term plan, or the annual plan for this year and the next two years, they should be realistic. Of course, fighting against the right-leaning conservatives is a major task and we cannot throw cold water onto enthusiastic masses. However, when the leaders are hotheaded, using cold water to wash may help them keep a cool head (Zhou, 1984, p. 191).

Clearly, the policy differences between Mao and Zhou started to surface as they set divergent policy tones. At that time, the primary economic problem was that the shortage of raw materials and limited production capacity were at odds with the high targets in capital investment. Recognizing this problem, Zhou Enlai, Chen Yun, and Bo Yibo all advocated cooling down the economy. At a Politburo meeting held in late April, Mao urged the State Council to increase

---

[11] Zhongguo Gongchandang Diqijie Zhongyang Weiyuanhui Diliuci Quanti Huiyi Guanyu Nongye Hezuohua Wenti de Jueyi (The Sixth Plenary Session of the Seventh Central Committee of the Communist Party of China's Resolution on the Issue of Agricultural Cooperativeness). October 11, 1955. www.gov.cn/test/2008-06/02/content_1002944.htm

[12] People's Daily. January 1, 1956. "Wei Quanmian de Tizao Wancheng he Chao'e Wancheng Wunian Jihua er Fendou" (Struggle for the Early Completion and Over-Completion of the Five-Year Plan).

capital investment by two billion RMB for the year 1956, yet his proposal was met with opposition from several leaders, most notably Zhou Enlai, ultimately leading to Mao's outrage (Jin, 2015, p. 1109).

In June 1956, the State Council began to cut the budget and lower planning targets, eventually putting forward the guideline of "opposing both conservatism and adventurism" (*ji fan baoshou, you fan maojin*), which was endorsed and supported by Liu Shaoqi. To support the State Council, Liu Shaoqi instructed the Propaganda Department to draft out an editorial on the *People's Daily* to set a policy tone. On June 20, 1956, the *People's Daily* published an editorial entitled "We not only Oppose Conservatism but also Oppose Impatient Mindsets," emphasizing that "When opposing conservative ideas, we should not neglect or diminish our opposition to impetuous and adventurous tendencies. Only by opposing both right-leaning conservative ideas and impetuous and adventurous ideas can we move forward in the right direction."[13]

In fact, prior to its publication, Mao circled his name and wrote the words on the finalized proof of this editorial: "I will not read it" (*bu kan le*) (Bo, 1991, p. 556). Mao was furious about this editorial when it was published. At the Nanning conference in 1958, Mao harshly criticized this editorial and believed that it was specifically directed towards him: "Who was this editorial directed at? It was a criticism of my preface to *Surge* (*gao chao*). The editorial proposed a policy that was not conducive to socialist construction, and did not consider it would create such an anti-adventurism atmosphere and dampen enthusiasm" (Feng and Jin, 2013, pp. 1737–1738).

Despite Mao's dissatisfaction, anti-adventurism (*fan maojin*) became a policy guideline in the latter half of 1956. Zhou Enlai and other central planners began to work on the revision of the Second Five-Year Plan, in an effort to lower development targets. In the end, Mao made a compromise at a Politburo meeting in July and endorsed a reasonable and realistic plan in September (Shen, 2008). The Eighth Party Congress in September 1956 adhered to the general policy direction of economic development, which was to oppose both conservatism and adventurism and to make steady progress in a comprehensive and balanced manner. In particular, Zhou Enlai's report at the Eighth Party Congress emphasized that "according to the needs and possibilities, the pace of development of the national economy should be reasonably set, and that the plan should be built on a positive and solid foundation to ensure a more balanced development of the national economy" (Zhou, 1984, p. 218). In a sense, the criticism

---

[13] *People's Daily*, June 20, 1956. Yao Fandui Baoshou Zhuyi, Yeyao Fandui Jizao Qingxu (We not only Oppose Conservatism but also Oppose Impatient Mindsets).

of adventurism and the abandonment of overambitious economic plans suggested that Mao encountered a setback in this round of policy disputes with State Council planners (MacFarquhar, 1974).

At the Third Plenary Session of the Eighth Party Congress in October 1957, however, Mao began to strike back. Mao made a speech entitled "Be the Promoters of the Revolution" (*zuo geming de cujinpai*) and harshly criticized the anti-adventurism:

> Last year, we swept away several things. One was sweeping away "more, faster, better, and more economically." People do not want 'more' and do not want 'faster.' As for the 'better' and 'more economically', they had also been swept away in the meantime. I think no one was opposed to 'better' and 'more economically,' it was just 'more' and 'faster' that some people didn't like, and some comrades called them 'adventurism' (*mao*)...We are talking about "more, faster, better and more economically" in a practical and realistic manner, rather than in the realm of subjectivism (*zhuguan zhuyi*). We should always strive for a little bit 'more' and a little bit 'faster,' just oppose the so-called 'more' and 'faster' associated with subjectivism. An ill wind swept away this slogan in the second half of last year, and I would like to restore it. Is it possible? Folks, please study it (Mao, 1977, p. 474).

On December 12, 1957, Mao drafted an editorial entitled "We Must Adhere to the Development Guideline of More, Faster, Better, More Economically" in the *People's Daily*. In this editorial, Mao strongly condemned those in the camp of "anti-adventurism":

> For a period of time after last autumn, a gust of wind blew among certain departments, certain units, and certain cadres, and the policy of 'more, faster, better and more economically' was surprisingly blown away. As a result, things that should have been done more and quickly were done less, slower or even not done. Of course, this kind of practice cannot play a positive role in promoting socialist construction, on the contrary it plays a negative role in 'promoting retreat.'[14]

Furthermore, at the Nanning conference in January 1958, Mao set a tone by stating, "Do not mention the term 'anti-adventurism' any more, it is a political issue" (Feng and Jin, 2013, p. 1734). Mao continued to argue that "the anti-adventurism in 1956 discouraged 600 million people, and it was a wrong policy guideline" (Feng and Jin, 2013, p. 1734). Mao publicly criticized the State Council planners, particularly Zhou Enlai and Chen Yun, accusing them of having "brought themselves to within 50 meters of the Rightists"

---

[14] *People's Daily*, June 20, 1956. *Bixu Jianchi duo kuai hao sheng de Jianshe Fangzhen* (We Must Adhere to the Development Guideline of More, Faster, Better, More Economically).

(Feng and Jin, 2013, p. 1734). Liu Shaoqi, Zhou Enlai, and Chen Yun all had to do self-criticism at the meeting. Perhaps more importantly, Mao criticized the decentralism (*fensan zhuyi*) of the State Council:

> I have not read the report to the National People's Congress for two years ... Zhang Bojun said that the State Council only provided finished products and did not allow participation in the design. I sympathize with him.[15] However, he represents the bourgeois political design institute (*zichan jieji zhengzhi shejiyuan*), while we are the proletarian political design institute (*wuchan jieji zhengzhi shejiyuan*). Some people come with finished products just before the meeting starts the next day, which is equivalent to forcing us to sign ... You usually don't communicate with us, don't give us any semi-finished products or raw materials, and you have to wait until everything is done before giving them to us. This is actually a blockade for us. Many documents are signed with eyes closed ... When reporting work, we need to leave the notebook and discuss the problems, present the main ideas, and explain why we have to do it this way and not that way. The economic and financial ministries do not report to the Politburo, and the reports are generally not easy to discuss (Li, 1996, pp. 77–78).

During this period, Mao Zedong's criticism of the State Council's decentralism primarily referred to instances where the State Council handled important matters without seeking approval from the Party center or reporting to the Party center in a timely manner, thus undermining the centralized and unified leadership of the Party. Mao also voiced his discontent with the concentration of power in the State Council and advocated for the Party center to assume a more dominant role:

> The Party center has only grasped power in two specific domains: one is revolution and the other is agriculture, with other real powers residing in the State Council. Some people oppose the fusion of Party and government, and want to seize more power, leaving the Party committees with minor powers. Even with the best intentions, they want to seize half of the major powers. In this way, there is no centralization. Centralization can only be achieved within the Party committees, the Politburo, the Secretariat, and the Standing Committee, and there can only be one core. (Li, 1996, p. 79).

In essence, Mao complained that the Politburo had become a "rubber stamp," which was similar to "Dulles's United Nations" (MacFarquhar, 1983, p. 26).

---

[15] Zhang Bojun was the Chairman of Chinese Peasants' and Workers' Democratic Party and Vice Chairman of the China Democratic League. He also held the position of Minister of Transportation from 1949 to 1958. During the Hundred Flowers Campaign, he advocated that democratic parties in China should become one of the political design institutes in shaping the country's political landscape. During the Anti-Rightist Campaign in 1957, he was labelled as "China's number one rightist."

As moderate economic policies were condemned and abandoned, the Nanning conference actually sounded the horn for the Great Leap Forward. Starting in early 1958, the central government and the provinces began revising their initially pragmatic plan targets. In an effort to display political loyalty to the Party leadership and higher-level governments, each layer of government imposed increasingly high targets, which ultimately resulted in the catastrophic Great Leap Forward and the subsequent Great Famine (e.g., Dikötter, 2010; Liu, Shih, and Zhang, 2022; Yang, 1996).

3.3 Decentralization and Its Rapid Reversal during the Great Leap Forward

Mao orchestrated the Great Leap Forward to decentralize the administrative and economic authority to local governments and mobilize local initiatives to achieve rapid economic growth. Mao decided to launch the Great Leap Forward in part to "achieve the requisite political dominance over the economic bureaucracy" (MacFarquhar, 1983, p. 27). Decentralization policies could have helped Mao consolidate his hold on power. By diminishing and diluting the authority of political leaders and technocrats in the central government, the authoritarian ruler would have faced less contestation and challenge from the central leadership, resulting in a relative increase in his power.[16] In the meantime, decentralization also empowers subnational and local governments, which can serve as allies of the paramount leader to counterbalance the vested interests of the central government.[17]

---

[16] Chenggang Xu made a similar point in an op-ed article published in the *Financial Times*. See: *Financial Times (Chinese)*, October 24, 2016, "The Institutional Roots of the Cultural Revolution and the Resulting Institutional Changes" (Wenge de Zhidu Genyuan jiqi Daozhi de Zhidu Bianhua), www.ftchinese.com/story/001069821?full=y&archive. By similar logic, in the 1980s, top leaders such as Zhao Ziyang and Hu Yaobang employed the strategy of "playing to the provinces" (Shirk, 1993). Shih (2008) notes that in the power competition between Party generalists and central technocrats in the central leadership, Party generalists tend to decentralize economic power to local officials to win their political support.

[17] At the Nanning Conference, Mao Zedong praised the enthusiasm of local officials in developing the economy, using it as evidence against the anti-adventurism while criticizing the leadership of the State Council. On January 25, 1958, the *People's Daily* published an editorial titled "Ride the Wind and Waves and Accelerate the Construction of a New Socialist Shanghai" (Chengfengpolang, Jiasu Jianshe Shehui Zhuyi xin Shanghai), which was based on a report by Ke Qingshi, the Party Secretary of Shanghai, in December 1957. The article provided a clear and timely support for Mao's "More, Faster, Better, More Economically" policy guideline, while also furnishing him with ammunition to criticize anti-adventurism. During the Nanning Conference, Mao Zedong spoke highly of Ke Qingshi's article on the *People's Daily* and asked Premier Zhou Enlai if he had read it and could write something similar, to which Zhou Enlai replied that he had read it but was unable to write like that (Li, 1996, p. 63). In May 1958, Ke Qingshi was promoted as a Politburo member at the Fifth Plenum of the Eighth Party Congress.

In the 1950s, Mao had been grappling with the ever-growing power of the central elites and bureaucracy. He had been considering strategies to restore a balance of power between the central and local governments. In April 1956, Mao delivered a famous speech entitled "On the Ten Major Relationships" (*lun shida guanxi*) during an enlarged session of a Politburo meeting. With respect to the relationship between the central and local authorities, Mao pointed out:

> The relationship between the central and the local authorities constitutes another contradiction (*maodun*). To resolve this contradiction, given the unified and consolidated leadership of the central authorities, our attention should now be focused on how to augment the powers of the local authorities to some extent, grant them greater independence and let them do more. This will be beneficial to our task of building a powerful socialist country (Mao, 1997, p. 31).

A few days later, in a concluding speech, Mao discussed the historical lessons of the CCP regarding centralization and decentralization and expressed his concerns about the concentration of power in central authorities and the lack of local autonomy in the 1950s:

> In recent years, however, there has been a tendency towards too much centralization. Some issues, such as the concentration of industry, how much autonomy the factories should have, how much autonomy the agricultural production cooperatives should have, how much autonomy the localities should have, have not yet been studied (Mao, 1997, p. 52).

Furthermore, Mao urged Zhou Enlai and the State Council to work with local officials to formulate a plan to resolve the relationship between the central and local authorities.

By the end of 1957, the targets set forth in the First Five-Year Plan had been successfully achieved. The entire country was filled with immense pride over this economic accomplishment and held even higher expectations for future development. In early 1958, Mao expressed his views on China's economic institutions:

> Too much centralized power is a constraint on the productive forces. This is the problem of the relationship between the superstructure and the economic base. I have always advocated for a 'titular monarchical republic' *(xujun gonghe)* and the central government should do some things, but not too many. The bulk of things should be delegated to provinces and cities. They can do a better job than us. We should trust them...Each sector – industry, agriculture (initially local), finance, commerce, and culture and education – should all be decentralized (Bo, 1991, p. 796).

During the Great Leap Forward, the first wave of decentralization took place in China. In April 1958, the Central Committee of the CCP and the State Council issued a document titled "Several Provisions on the Decentralization of Industrial Enterprises" (*Gongye Qiye Xiafang de Jixiang Guiding*). The document stipulated that enterprises administered by the State Council "should, in principle, be decentralized and under local control, with some exceptions of certain major, special and 'experimental' enterprises."[18] Strikingly, 8,100 of the 9,300 centrally administered enterprises, constituting approximately 87 percent, were delegated to local governments in this wave of decentralization (Wu, 2016, p. 149).

The fiscal system witnessed a decentralization reform to enhance the fiscal capacity of local governments. Prior to 1958, the fiscal system was "Using Expenditure to Determine Revenues" (*yi zhi ding shou*), meaning that the central government determined the local expenditure each year, then allocated certain revenue items to the local authorities and set the revenue-sharing ratio. In 1958, the fiscal system was changed to "Using Revenues to Determine Expenditure" (*yi shou ding zhi*), meaning that the central government first determined the local fiscal revenue items and revenue-sharing ratio, and then the local authorities arranged expenditures based on their revenues.

To ensure that all levels of the government could formulate development plans in line with the Second Five-Year Plan, the fiscal reform also stipulated that the scope of local fiscal revenue and expenditure, income items, and the revenue-sharing ratio would remain fixed for a period of five years. In effect, the fiscal system of "Using Revenues to Determine Expenditure, No Change for Five Years" (*yi shou ding zhi, wunian bubian*) was established in 1958 (Xiang, 2006, p. 51). However, in 1959, the Chinese government introduced a fiscal system known as "Total Revenue Sharing, Change Once a Year" (*zong'e fencheng, yinian yibian*) with the goal of reducing the discretionary financial resources of local governments while continuing to decentralize revenue and expenditure to them. Under this system, most tax revenue sources were distributed between the central and local governments based on a predetermined sharing ratio which was ratified by the central authority on a annual basis, though a few selected taxes were handed over to the central government (Xiang, 2006, p. 52).

In addition, the planning management system underwent decentralization in China during the late 1950s. In September 1958, an official document titled

---

[18] Zhongguo Gongchandang Zhongyangweiyuanhui Guowuyuan Guanyu Gongye Qiye Xiafang de Jixiang Guiding (The Central Committee of the CCP and the State Council's Several Provisions on the Decentralization of Industrial Enterprises). April 11, 1958. www.gov.cn/gongbao/shuju/1958/gwyb195814.pdf (accessed on February 3, 2023).

"Provisions on Improving the Planning Management System" (*Guanyu Gaijin Jihua Guanli Tizhi de Guiding*) was issued by the central leadership. These provisions essentially gave local governments greater economic autonomy in a centrally planned economy. Specifically, local governments were granted the authority to adjust the production targets for industry and agriculture in their jurisdictions, determine the scale and investment of local construction projects, allocate and transfer local production materials, and utilize surpluses exceeding designated production quotas.[19] Consequently, the number of production materials distributed by the State Planning Commission and administered by the ministries of the State Council declined significantly, from 530 in 1957 to 132 in 1959 (Wu, 2016, p. 48). This shift in planning authority enabled local governments to have greater control over the allocation of production materials.

Furthermore, the central government decentralized the approval process for capital construction projects. For local construction projects exceeding a certain limit, only a brief plan book needed to be submitted to the central government for approval, while other design and budget documents were reviewed and approved by the local government; for projects below a certain limit, the local government had complete decision-making authority (Wu, 2016, p. 48). This decentralization policy granted local governments greater authority in managing capital construction projects within their respective jurisdictions. In July 1958, a system of investment contracting (*touzi baogan*) was introduced for local construction projects, replacing the previous method of funding all construction investments through state allocations for specific purposes. This allowed local governments to undertake a diverse range of projects within the total amount of funds allocated by the central government and locally raised funds (Wu, 2016, p. 48).

The Great Leap Forward had a profound and devastating impact on China's economy. The policies implemented during this period ultimately resulted in a catastrophic collapse in grain production and a widespread famine across the country from 1959 to 1961.[20] In January 1961, the Ninth Plenary Session of the Eighth CCP Central Committee officially decided to implement the policy of "adjusting, consolidating, enriching, and improving"

---

[19] Zhonggong Zhongyang Guowuyuan Guanyu Gaijin Jihua Guanli Tizhi de Guiding (The Central Committee of the CCP and the State Council's Provisions on Improving the Planning Management System). September 24, 1958. In *Zhonggong Zhongyang Wenjian Xuanji, di ershijiu ce (Selected Documents of the Chinese Communist Party Central Committee: Volume 29)*, ed. The Central Party Archives. Beijing: Central Party School Publisher. pp. 82–86.

[20] The estimated excess deaths of the Great Famine in China range from a minimum of 15 million to a maximum of 30 million (e.g., Ashton et al., 1984; Coale, 1981).

(*tiaozhen, gonggu, chongshi, tigao*) for the national economy. The Great Leap Forward came to an end.

In the same month, the Party center issued a document outlining provisions to revamp the economic management system. The document stipulated that economic management authority should be centralized to the central government and the central bureaus within the next two to three years.[21] Local or provincial plans would be arranged by the Central Bureaus under the unified leadership of the central government. Additionally, the administrative management, production oversight, material distribution, and cadre management of enterprises directly affiliated with the central ministries would be controlled and managed by the central ministries. The document also emphasized the need to centralize financial authority, balance budgetary revenues and expenditures at all levels, prohibit deficit budgets, and rectify off-budget revenue and expenditure.[22]

In January 1962, Liu Shaoqi criticized "decentralism" (*fensan zhuyi*) at the 7,000 Cadres Conference:

> Decentralization has been too much and has led to a severe proliferation of decentralist tendencies ... This in turn has damaged the unified leadership in economic life and undermined the state ownership system ... This decentralism in economic work has rendered the state incapable of formulating a unified and reasonable plan, and has disrupted the state's production plans, capital construction plans, material distribution plans, commercial plans, labor plans, and financial plans (Liu, 1985, pp. 349–417).

In the same speech, Liu Shaoqi put forth the following policy proposals to centralize economic authority: Local plans must be integrated into the national plan, and any modifications or expansions to these plans must be approved by the central government; all major industrial enterprises producing goods for national distribution must fall under the direct supervision of the central

---

[21] The central bureaus functioned as the representative agencies of the CCP's Central Committee at the regional level. During the early 1950s, six regional bureaus were established, namely the North Bureau, Central South Bureau, East Bureau, Northeast Bureau, Northwest Bureau, and Southwest Bureau. These bureaus were tasked with supervising several provinces or administrative areas. After the Gao-Rao Affair, the central leadership abolished the central bureaus and instead made Party committees at the provincial level directly accountable to the Party center. In January 1961, the Ninth Plenary Session of the Eighth Party Congress approved the restoration of the six central bureaus to reinforce the Party's leadership over the Party committees at the provincial and local levels. However, during the Cultural Revolution, the six central bureaus were abolished again.

[22] *Guanyu Tiaozheng Guanli Tizhi de Ruangan Zanxing Guiding* (Several Interim Provisions of the Central Committee on Adjusting the Management System). January 20, 1961. In *Jianguo yilai zhongyao wenxian xuanbian (Di Shisi Ce) (Selected Important Documents since the Founding of the People's Republic of China: Volume 14)*, ed. The CCP Party Literature Research Office. Beijing: The Central Literature Publishing House. pp. 102–105.

government, and those enterprises that have already been decentralized to local authorities must be gradually brought back under central control by 1962; all infrastructure projects and investments, regardless of being under central or local jurisdiction, must be included in the national plan, and no infrastructure projects or investments that fall outside the national plan will be permitted (Liu, 1985, p. 392).

Immediately after the 7,000 Cadres Conference, economic planners convened the Xilou conference in late February 1962. Chen Yun's speech at this conference laid out an economic recovery plan and called for greater central control "to prevent provincial foot-dragging" (MacFarquhar, 1997, p. 190). On February 26th, Li Xiannian, the Minister of Finance, emphasized the importance of financial discipline and warned against the misuse of the newly granted financial authorities by provincial and local governments during the Great Leap Forward (MacFarquhar, 1997, p. 195). This conference led to a widespread consensus that greater central control was imperative. The Ministry of Finance, denounced by Mao at the Nanning Conference prior to the Great Leap Forward, reclaimed its primary role in economic policymaking (MacFarquhar, 1997). Following the 7,000 Cadres Conference in 1962, Mao opted to retreat to the second line and left Beijing for South China. Mao would no longer be in charge of day-to-day work, which would be presided over by the State Chairman, Liu Shaoqi, and the General Secretary of the Secretariat, Deng Xiaoping.

As part of the push toward economic centralization, Liu Shaoqi, in the early 1960s, advocated for the establishment of giant "corporate trusts" (*tuo-lasi*) to coordinate industrial production on a national scale. The national- and regional-wide corporate trusts recentralized industrial production, fiscal authority, and personnel control, leading to inevitable tensions between local governments and enterprises (Bo, 1991, pp. 1220–1221). For instance, the merger of local enterprises into corporate trusts, owing to their good financial performance, would inevitably lead to a decline in local fiscal revenue upon the transfer of control to the central government. During the Cultural Revolution, Liu Shaoqi's policy of "corporate trusts" was denounced as "dictatorship by central ministries" (*tiaotiao zhuanzheng*): "Using the pretext of opposing decentralization, they overemphasized centralization, promoted 'highly monopolized' industries, established capitalist trusts, stressed vertical leadership, imposed top-down control, implemented 'dictatorship by central ministries,' and stifled the enthusiasm of local governments for industrial development."[23] Interestingly, when Deng Xiaoping was being criticized during the

---

[23] *People's Daily*, May 28, 1970. "Difang Xiaoxing Gongye de Fanzhan Daolu" (The Development Path of Local Small-Scale Industry).

Cultural Revolution, the practice of "dictatorship by central ministries" was singled out for its tendency to "undermine the authority of the Party center, suppress local authorities, neither trusting the Party nor the masses, with only a small group of people within the central ministries (*tiaotiao*) who made key decisions."[24] This criticism highlights the concern of the Party leadership, particularly Mao, about the expansion of bureaucratic power and its potential to subvert the Party and Mao's goals.

The preceding historical analysis reveals that the roots of both fiscal and enterprise decentralization can be traced back to the Great Leap Forward, which was initiated in 1958. These observations align with previous scholarly work of Donnithorne and Lardy (1976), Naughton (1988), Oksenberg and Tong (1991), and Xu (2011). Nonetheless, it is important to note that this period of decentralization was short-lived, as a recentralization process took shape in the early 1960s.

From the political economy perspective, we analyze this wave of decentralization and recentralization by examining the elite composition of the ruling party in China. We begin our analysis with the composition of the Central Committee (CC) at the 1956 Eighth Party Congress, which selected the CC members for the subsequent thirteen years. Upon investigating the composition of the Central Committee's elite during the Eighth Party Congress, it appears that the recentralization process was facilitated by the notable presence of a large majority of central officials among the political elite at that time. Figure 2 presents a dynamic depiction of the proportion of central, military, and provincial officials in the Central Committee.

From the Eighth Party Congress in 1956 to the onset of the Cultural Revolution in 1966, central officials constituted the overwhelming majority in the Central Committee. According to our definition, the central share of CC members remained relatively stable at around 75 percent during this period. Using a broader definition, the central share of the CC reached approximately 80 percent in most years. In contrast, local political elites found themselves marginalized in the Eighth Party Congress, and this disadvantage endured until the Cultural Revolution.[25]

Given the dominance of central officials in this period, it was not surprising that Great Leap decentralization policies were rapidly reversed after 1960.

---

[24] *People's Daily*, September 8, 1976. "Deng Xiaoping Chonggao Tiaotiao Zhuanzheng de Fandong Benzhi" (The Reactionary Essence of Deng Xiaoping's Restoration of Dictatorship by Central Ministries).

[25] There was a slight increase in the share of local officials after the Great Leap Forward when Peng Dehuai and a few other central officials – including Cheng Zihua, Li Xuefeng, Liu Lantao, and Wang Shoudao – were purged or dispatched to provincial positions.

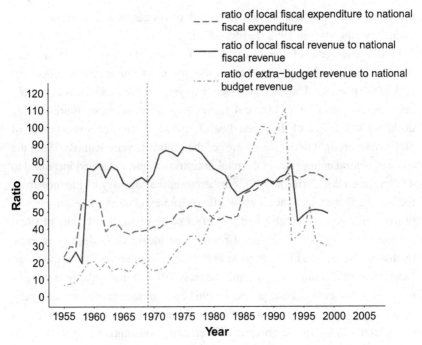

Figure 4 Ratio of local expenditure, local revenue, and extrabudgetary revenue (%).
Source: China Statistical Yearbook (Various Years)

In Figure 4, the local share of total revenue and expenditure surged during the Great Leap Forward in 1958 and remained at that level until the late 1970s, when it began to decline. As discussed earlier, China initiated fiscal decentralization in 1957, which devolved control of nearly all state-owned enterprises (SOEs) to the local levels, shifted economic planning from the central to the local levels, and implemented revenue-sharing agreements between the center and provinces. The results were breath-taking: The share of central revenue likewise decreased from 75 percent to below 50 percent (see Figure 4). The share of industrial output produced by central SOEs – those affiliated with the central government – shrank from 39.7 percent to 13.8 percent (Wu, 2016, p. 149).

The decentralization coincided with the Great Leap Forward and was an integral part of Mao's strategy to spur local enthusiasm for increasing production (Donnithorne and Lardy, 1976). Despite impressive official figures showing considerable fiscal decentralization, the reality was much more complex. First, as Lardy shows, the central authorities still tightly controlled expenditure so that provinces which collected more revenue did not spend more than before the decentralization (Lardy, 1975). Furthermore, although the center initially pledged to set revenue sharing rates with provinces for five years, it reneged on this promise in 1959 and set new rates with provinces in accordance with the budgetary outcomes in 1958 (Lardy, 1975).

In the aftermath of the Great Leap Forward, the central government reclaimed much of its power even as the provinces continued to collect the bulk of the revenue. Thus, the provinces enjoyed little de facto fiscal autonomy between 1961 and 1970. Figure 4 shows local share of expenditure sharply declining at the end of the Great Leap Forward. A considerable number of SOEs were brought under the control of the central government. By 1965, the share of central enterprises in the total industrial output value had increased to 42.2 percent (Wu, 2016, p. 149). Furthermore, the Ministry of Finance froze the extrabudgetary bank accounts of all governmental units and enterprises to prevent inflation, which also had the effect of depriving local units of fiscal autonomy (Xiang, 1999). Figure 4 reveals that local extrabudgetary revenue relative to the national budget froze at the same level at the end of the Great Leap Forward and did not grow until the early 1970s. Finally, the launching of the Third Front construction project in 1964 concentrated enormous budgetary funds in the hands of central authorities to focus on key construction projects (Naughton, 1988). In the absence of a credible constitution and with a ruling bloc dominated by central officials, the rapid recentralization seen in the post–Great Leap period was fully expected.

3.4 Credible Decentralization: Removal of Central Officials from the CC

The second, more enduring wave of decentralization began in 1970. Although this wave of decentralization had much in common with the 1958 decentralization, the level of decentralization was deeper and longer lasting. In the aftermath of the Great Leap Forward, elite conflicts in the early 1960s sowed the seeds for the Cultural Revolution, ultimately resulting in this second wave of decentralization as an unintended consequence.

The tension between Mao and Liu Shaoqi shifted into high gear after the 1962 7,000 Cadres Conference, when both Liu and his followers criticized Mao for the errors committed during the disastrous Great Leap Forward. In Liu Shaoqi's oral report at the 7,000 Cadres Conference, Liu Shaoqi implied that the causes of the economic hardships could be attributed to "30% natural calamities and 70% human-induced disasters" and concluded that, "speaking of the whole country, the relationship between shortcomings and achievements cannot be described as one finger to nine fingers, but rather, it is probably a relationship of three fingers to seven fingers" (Liu, 1985, pp. 419–421). When preparing the report for the 7,000 Cadres Conference, Peng Zhen, Liu's follower in the

Northern Bureau during the 1930s, said, "Currently, there is a tendency within the Party where people are afraid to offer opinions and review mistakes. They believe that engaging in such a review would lead to the collapse of the Party. If even 1% or 0.1% of Chairman Mao's mistakes are not examined and addressed, it will leave a detrimental impact on our Party" (Bo, 1991, p. 1026).

Mao sensed that Liu not only failed to actively support his leadership but also seemed to be subtly "pressuring" him. In February 1967, when meeting with Hysni Kapo and Beqir Balluku from the Albanian delegation, Mao touched on the connection between the 7,000 Cadres Conference and the Cultural Revolution: "At the 7,000 Cadres Conference I said that the revisionists wanted to overthrow us and if we did not pay attention, if we did not fight back, then in at least a few years, or maybe ten, and at most a few decades, China would become a fascist dictatorship. At that time, I pointed out this issue" (Feng and Jin, 2013, p. 45). In April 1967, Jiang Qing once said that Chairman Mao had been holding his breath with anger (*bie le yikouqi*) at the 7,000 Cadres Conference and it was not until the Cultural Revolution that he finally let out this breath (Zhang, 2006, p. 281).

In the wake of the 7,000 Cadres Conference, Mao made a speech at the 10th Plenum of the Eighth Party Congress in September 1962 and emphasized the importance of class struggle again: "[We] must recognize the protracted nature of the existence of classes, recognize the struggle of class against class ... Hence, from this moment on, we must talk about it every year, every month, every day" (Teiwes, 1984, p. 21). In 1963, Mao launched the nationwide Socialist Education Movement, also known as the "Four Cleanups" Movement. Toward the end of 1963, Liu Shaoqi shifted his focus to promoting this movement. In November, he directed his wife, Wang Guangmei, to participate in the "Four Cleanups" campaign in Hebei Province. After a five-month stay in Taoyuan Brigade, Wang Guangmei presented her report at a Hebei Provincial Party Committee meeting in July 1964. Following this, she accompanied Liu Shaoqi to more than ten provinces across the country, where she delivered the same report. In August, Liu held a meeting with cadres in the upper echelons of the CCP and urged them to learn from Wang Guangmei by conducting on-the-ground investigations. He asserted that engaging in such fieldwork was a prerequisite for holding positions as a Central Committee member, provincial party secretary, or local party secretary. It was widely known among the CCP's upper echelons that Liu had conducted on-the-ground investigations in his hometown in Hunan in 1961, while Mao had never done so. Furthermore, Liu dismissed the practice of convening investigation meetings (diaocha hui), an approach favored by Mao, contending that they could not capture the true situation in the countryside, where local cadres often had problems. After this meeting, Jiang Qing approached Mao in tears, lamenting, "Even though Khrushchev only presented a secret report after Stalin passed away, they are giving an open report now, while you are still alive" (Wang, 2001, p. 573). When the Central Committee distributed Wang Guangmei's report in September, Liu remarked, "The experience gained in Taoyuan Brigade holds universal significance," resulting in its extensive circulation (Feng and Jin, 2013, p. 2322). The enormous influence and top-down mobilization capacity wielded by Liu aroused Mao's suspicion. In the summer of 1964, at Liu's strong urging, nearly two million cadres nationwide were mobilized to participate in the "Four Cleanups" campaign across both urban and rural areas (MacFarquhar, 1997, p. 430).

During a Politburo Committee work meeting on December 20, 1964, a severe clash erupted between Mao and Liu. Mao emphasized the importance of addressing the issue of capitalist roaders in power within the Party's higher echelons, maintaining that the key problem lay with high-level cadres rather than grassroots team leaders or branch secretaries. Mao contended: "First, deal with the jackals and wolves; then, deal with the foxes. This is how we grasp the problem. You must start with those in power, or it won't work" (Feng and Jin, 2013, p. 2357). He criticized Liu's approach as "leftist on the surface" but actually protecting the capitalist roaders. Furthermore, Mao asserted that there were two factions within the Party: the socialist faction and the capitalist faction (Feng and Jin, 2013, p. 2340), clearly signaling his distrust of Liu. From the second half of 1965 onward, Mao lost his interest in the "Four Cleanups" Movement, believing that it could not address the fundamental problem, and began contemplating the launch of another political campaign, the Cultural Revolution (Bo, 1991, p. 1135).

In terms of economic policies, Mao expressed discontent with the economic centralization policies enacted by the central government following the 7,000 Cadres Conference. After he retreated to the second line, he was frustrated by the increasingly bureaucratized and routinized Party machine so that he later complained that he was treated as "a dead ancestor" and "Deng Xiaoping never came to consult me" (Meisner, 1999, p. 254). In January 1964, Mao commented on giant corporate trusts: "The current method of managing the economy through administrative means is not good and needs to be changed" (Gu, 1993, p. 589). In September 1964, Mao criticized the government's economic work, expressing concern that "in the past there was too much decentralization and everything was delegated, but now the central government is exerting too much control" (Gu, 1993, p. 610).

In a letter to Liu Shaoqi on March 12, 1966, Mao wrote:

Therefore, raw material (steel), work machines, and agricultural machinery should be subject to national management. If local production exceeds the national plan by a significant margin (such as more than double) or exceeds the allocated quota, it should be permitted to retain 30% to 50% for local purchase and use. Without this rule, local initiatives cannot be effectively mobilized ... When everything is centralized under the central authority, strictly controlled, it is not a good approach (Mao, 1998, pp. 19–20).

In the following Politburo meeting at Hangzhou on March 20, Mao emphasized the importance of decentralization again:

The accumulation of resources at the local level should be encouraged, and not all resources should be concentrated at the central level, as this would hinder the expansion of local reproduction. The Soviet Union suffered from this mistake. Currently, stifling people's initiative and implementing rigid top-down control hinders the development of productivity, and it is reactionary. It would be better if the central government were to become a 'titular monarchical republic,' focusing only on major policies, guidelines, and plans ... In summary, control should not be overly rigid. Restrictions are necessary but should not be suffocating. Whether it is expanding agricultural production or industrial production, attention must be paid to the distribution of power between the central and local governments. We cannot drain the pond to catch all the fish (Feng and Feng, 2013b, p. 569).

Clearly, in the mid-1960s, Mao became dissatisfied with post-Stalin Soviet policies and "was unwilling to permit his party-state to evolve into a stable bureaucracy ruled by bureaucrats who lorded over subordinates and paid lip service to revolutionary ideals, but were motivated by career advancement and material comfort" (Walder, 2015, pp. 121–122). In May 1966, an "enlarged session" of the Politburo released the "May 16 Notification" to middle and high-level party cadres, accusing "counter-revolutionary revisionists" of infiltrating the Party, indicating that there were enemies within the Party itself.[26]

On August 5, during the 11th Plenary Session of the Eighth Party Congress, Mao authored *Bombard the Headquarters – My Big-Character Poster*, in which he accused leading comrades of obstructing the Great Cultural Revolution of the proletariat.[27] Although not explicitly named, Liu Shaoqi and Deng Xiaoping were widely seen as the "bourgeois headquarters" and were

---

[26] *People's Daily*, May 17, 1967. "Zhongguo Gongchandang Zhongyang Weiyuanhui Tongzhi" (The Notification of the CCP Central Committee). This notification was a secret inner-party document and was published in *People's Daily* one year after its initial circulation within the Party.

[27] *People's Daily*, August 5, 1967. "Paoda Silingbu – Wode Yizhang Dazibao" (Bombard the Headquarters – My Big-Character Poster). This article was published in *People's Daily* one year after its initial circulation within the Party.

subsequently sidelined from day-to-day party affairs. Mao's blueprint for the Cultural Revolution, the *Decision of the CCP Central Committee Concerning the Great Proletarian Cultural Revolution* published in *People's Daily* on August 9, pointed out that the objective was "to struggle against and overthrow those persons in authority who are taking the capitalist road," unleashing mass rebellion against the Party establishment.[28]

During the Cultural Revolution, students and industrial workers were mobilized to criticize state bureaucracies and officials with "revisionist" tendencies. The central Party apparatus was dismantled into small working groups, and the majority of Party cadres were purged, resulting in the cessation of civilian Party organizations by the end of 1966 (Walder, 2016). By the end of 1968, all of China's provinces and autonomous regions had established "revolutionary committees" (*ge wei hui*), consisting of surviving civilian officials, rebel leaders, and military officers. These committees were tasked with establishing similar structures at municipal and county levels, ultimately resulting in the practice of military dictatorship by the revolutionary committees (e.g., Dong and Walder, 2012).

As illustrated in Figures 2 and 3, the Cultural Revolution marked a turning point in the composition of the CC. With the onset of the Cultural Revolution, a substantial number of CC members working in central Party organs and the State Council were stripped of their CC membership. This political shock also was exogenous to economic policies and had to do with the political struggle between Mao and his designated successor Liu Shaoqi. Mao mobilized contingents of the People's Liberation Army (PLA) under Lin Biao and radical propaganda officials in Shanghai to unseat Liu and other potential rivals in 1966 (MacFarquhar, 1997; MacFarquhar and Schoenhals, 2006). Notably, on the eve of the Cultural Revolution, Liu's followers occupied over 40 percent of the Central Committee seats (Shih, Shan, and Liu, 2010a).

Thus, Mao's decision to eradicate his potential enemies inadvertently led to the decimation of the central bureaucracy. As depicted in Table 2, scores of ministers and vice ministers, including many who had previous ties with Liu, such as Cheng Zihua, Bo Yibo, Yang Yichen, Yang Xiufeng, and Zhang Linzhi, among others, were removed from the State Council at the outset of the Cultural Revolution. Naturally, they were not reelected into the CC at the 1969 Ninth Party Congress. Out of the twenty-two ministers who had been full or alternate CC members in 1965, thirteen were purged during the Cultural Revolution, and

---

[28] *People's Daily*, August 9, 1966. "Zhongguo Gongchandang Zhongyang Weiyuanhui Guanyu Wuchanjieji Wenhua dageming de Jueding" (The Decision of the CCP Central Committee concerning the Great Proletarian Cultural Revolution).

Table 2 Ministers in 1965 and Their fate during the Cultural Revolution

	Total Number	Purged	Purged (%)	Purged or Removed from the State Council	Purged or Removed from the State Council (%)
Ministers in 1965	49	28	57.14%	37	75.5%
CCP Member Ministers in 1965	41	26	63.41%	31	75.6%
Ministers in 1965 who were CC or ACC Members	22	13	59.09%	16	72.7%

Notes: If a minister regained his/her former position after 1970, he/she is not considered purged.

another two were transferred to provincial administration. Only six ministers in 1965 remained in power by the 1969 Ninth Party Congress.[29]

Why didn't Mao replace the ministers with his trusted followers who were high-ranking CC members? In brief, doing so would have served no political purpose for Mao. Mao launched the Cultural Revolution in part to eradicate increasingly powerful central state organs dominated by factions that challenged him. He was not interested in rebuilding them only to face the same threat again. Instead, Mao pursued a strategy of "coalitions of the weak" to consolidate his grip on power (Shih, 2022). In this strategy, the Central Cultural Revolution group, which consisted of his wife Jiang Qing and several "scribblers" such as Chen Boda, Zhang Chuanqiao, and Yaowen Yuan, largely controlled the Party apparatus. Li Xiannian, who had been accused of splitting the Party in the 1930s, came to dominate the remaining State Council offices as a Vice Premier and a Politburo member, although he was constantly under threat of being purged for his crimes thirty years before and thus did not dare to rebuild the State Council bureaucracy (Shih, 2022).

---

[29] The lucky few who regained entry into the Ninth CC included Minister of Defense Lin Biao, Minister of Public Security Xie Fuzhi, Minister of Foreign Affairs Chen Yi, State Planning Commission Head Li Fuchun, Minister of Finance Li Xiannian, and Director of the State Science and Technology Commission Minister Nie Rongzhen.

Because the military played a large part in pacifying the chaos in the provinces, military officers took over numerous important positions in the provinces when the revolutionary committees were formed to replace party committees (MacFarquhar and Schoenhals, 2006). Unlike central ministries, the new provincial military rulers tended to be high-prestige Mao loyalists or members of Mao's weak coalition. The decision to place military officers in provincial administration led to a rising presence of the military in the CC from 26 percent in 1968 to 52 percent in 1969. Only Lin Biao's purge in 1971 led to a decline in PLA representation back to around 40 percent.

Because Mao only needed to destroy the most threatening factions rather than all factions, provincial administrators, who had come from a much more diverse array of factions than central ministers, were not purged to the same extent as the central ministerial purge. Mao also decided to enlarge the CC by introducing scores of provincial mass representatives into the Ninth Central Committee, presumably to balance against the military (MacFarquhar and Schoenhals, 2006). For those in provincial and local authorities, including civilian officials and rebel leaders, their revolutionary credentials were not particularly strong, and their collective action capabilities were considerably limited. These relatively junior officials and rebel leaders primarily attributed their leadership positions to Mao's personal trust, resulting in their unwavering loyalty to him.

When political power was redistributed among different groups at the Ninth Party Congress in 1969, a fundamental shift in the power structure favoring decentralization had occurred. As illustrated in Figure 2, the central share of CC membership, calculated by the more restricted definition, plummeted from around 75 percent to below 30 percent. Figure 3 reveals that the share of State Council and central SOE CC members dropped considerably from 48 percent in 1965 to only 16 percent in 1969. Most notably, the Cultural Revolution saw the rise of the local political elite: the provincial share of CC membership soared from approximately 16 percent in 1968 to 49 percent in 1969 and reached its peak in 1973, as seen in Figures 2 and 3.

The radical reorientation of the political elite during the Cultural Revolution had a profound impact on the incentives of the top leaders. With the CC dominated by local officials, senior leaders who aimed to forge a winning coalition must ally with a sizable segment of provincial leaders. Naturally, their concerns and economic interests also became important considerations in top-level economic decision making. Although Mao may have preferred decentralization, his successors were committed to a path of decentralization because of an elite selectorate primarily dominated by local interests.

After the Ninth Party Congress, the provinces began to pursue drastic decentralization policies. In the fiscal realm, a lump-sum transfer system was adopted, devolving the bulk of fiscal resources to the local level (Oksenberg and Tong, 1991). Unlike the Great Leap Forward, the pursuit of decentralization after 1969 naturally drew strong support from an elite selectorate dominated by local officials, whereas centralization policies elicited opposition and foot-dragging. In 1971, the Ministry of Finance issued a directive regarding the establishment of a contract system for revenues and expenditures. Under this arrangement, certain revenue sources, including customs duties and central State-Owned Enterprise (SOE) revenue, were designated for the central government, while other sources, such as local SOE revenue, were classified as local revenue (Oksenberg and Tong, 1991). Importantly, fiscal surpluses were divided between the central and provincial governments according to prearranged agreements, and if there remained surplus after the agreed-upon remittance to the central government, provincial governments could retain all of it. More so than previous revenue-sharing arrangements, this system created strong incentives for local authorities to maximize revenue (Oksenberg and Tong, 1991). In 1972, the central government made adjustments to this system, stipulating that provinces could retain all excess revenues up to a limit of 100 million yuan, while any surplus revenue exceeding this amount had to be equally shared between the province and the central government (Xin, 2000, pp. 236–237).[30]

During 1974 and 1975, China introduced the "Fixed Ration Retention" (*guding bili liucheng*) fiscal system, which allowed provinces to retain a fixed proportion of fiscal revenue, with the retention ratio varying across provinces and averaging around 2.3 percent. Any surplus revenue was subject to a different ratio, typically not exceeding 30 percent. Local fiscal expenditures were contracted by quota, and year-end surpluses were retained for local use (Xin, 2000, p. 237). The objective of this new fiscal system was to enhance local fiscal capacity while improving the central government's overall fiscal balance. From 1976 to 1979, a system of "Linking Revenue with Expenditure, Sharing Total Revenue" (*shouzhi guagou, zong'e fencheng*) was put in place. This system maintained the established practice of fixed ratio retention of fiscal revenue and surplus revenue, while expanding the scope of local financial revenue and expenditure, ultimately providing local governments with some financial flexibility (Zhao, 1989, p. 244).

---

[30] The 1971 fiscal system encountered several challenges. For instance, under the fixed quota system, provinces could retain all fiscal surpluses, but provinces failing to meet their targets required subsidies from the central government, further straining the central government's fiscal balance.

In 1977, Jiangsu province initiated a pilot reform of the fiscal management system by adopting the "Fixed Ratio Contracting" (*guding bili fencheng*) system. Under this pilot system, Jiangsu province was granted the authority to determine the proportion of revenue to be remitted to the central government and the proportion to be retained, based on the ratio of budget expenditures to budget revenues in recent years, with the proportion remaining unchanged for a four-year period. Prior to the implementation of this system, the central government had stipulated the revenue to be remitted by Jiangsu province, with a proportion of 58 percent in 1978, which was subsequently raised to 61 percent. After fulfilling the required fiscal revenue remittance to the central government, Jiangsu province had the autonomy to allocate its retained revenue (Xin, 2000, p. 248). This approach incentivized local governments to actively pursue economic growth in order to generate greater fiscal revenue.

It is evident that China embarked on a trajectory of fiscal decentralization following the Ninth Party Congress in 1969. This wave of fiscal decentralization was closely associated with the growing influence of local officials within the Central Committee, suggesting a shift in political power dynamics. As illustrated in Figure 4, it was in the first half of the 1970s, and not the 1980s or 1990s as often believed, when localities obtained the highest share of revenue. Moreover, Figure 4 reveals that local extrabudgetary revenue, relative to the national budget, began to climb after the Ninth Party Congress. Notably, this trend of local fiscal autonomy was not reversed until the implementation of the tax-sharing system in 1994.

In the early 1970s, the decentralization of enterprises underwent a parallel trajectory to fiscal decentralization. Most large-scale SOEs were once again devolved to the control of provincial and local authorities. In February 1969, the National Planning Conference discussed the "Preliminary Ideas on the Decentralization of Enterprise Management System by Central Ministries" (*Zhongyang Gebu Guanyu Qiye Guanli Tizhi Xiafang de Chubu Shexiang*). The meeting concluded that, regarding the authority of "*tiaotiao*" (central ministries) and "*kuaikuai*" (regions) in economic management, the emphasis should be placed on "*kuaikuai*" and that unified leadership should be exercised by local revolutionary committees over enterprises (Feng and Feng, 2013a, p. 229). Subsequently, enterprises were gradually decentralized to local governments.

In 1970, a pronounced push was made toward the decentralization of enterprises. On March 5, the central government issued a directive requiring the ministries under the State Council to decentralize the majority of their directly affiliated enterprises to local management by the end of 1970; a small number of these enterprises would be jointly administrated by central ministries and local governments, with the local government taking the lead; and a very few large-scale or key enterprises would be jointly administrated by central ministries and local governments, with the central ministry taking the lead. Most SOEs were devolved to local governments at the provincial, municipal, and county levels. As a result, the number of central SOEs dropped from 10,533 in 1965 to approximately 1,600 in 1976, and their share of the total industrial output value declined from 42.2 percent to 6 percent (Zhao, 1989, p. 45). As Donnithorne (1972, p. 618) observes, the economic decentralization during the Cultural Revolution "strengthened tendencies towards a cellular pattern of development over much of the Chinese economy – those largely self-sufficient cells being either local authority units or enterprises."

An often discussed ingredient of China's rapid growth, commune and brigade enterprises (CBEs), which were the precursor of township and village enterprises (TVEs), also saw rapid expansion during the Cultural Revolution (e.g., Whiting, 2000; Zhang and Liu, 2019; Zhang et al., 2021).[31] In February 1970, the Fourth Five-Year Plan (draft) called for developing local "five small" industries (*wuxiao gongye*), which referred to small-scale rural enterprises at the local and county levels, encompassing small coal mines, small steel mills, small cement plants, small machinery factories, and small fertilizer plants. The central government planned to allocate eight billion yuan in special funds to support the development of local "five small" industries and formulate a series of preferential policies to encourage their growth. Notably, the plan stipulated that newly established county-run "five small" industries were entitled to retain 60 percent of their profits earned in the first two to three years; for "five small" industries that experienced temporary losses, the government could provide subsidies or tax deductions for a certain period of time, subject to the approval of the provincial, municipal, or district government; in cases of financial difficulties, banks or credit cooperatives could provide loans to support these industries ("Contemporary China's Economic Management" Compilation Group, 1996, p. 260). In August 1970, the State Council held a conference on the agriculture in northern China, where Premier Zhou Enlai suggested the acceleration of agricultural mechanization. In September of the following year, the State Council convened a national conference on agricultural mechanization, which established the development of collective enterprises and the implementation of rural industrialization as policy guidelines.

Consequently, the decentralization policy in the early 1970s fostered the development of CBEs in local "five small" industries. Consider, for example,

---

[31] In 1984, the term "commune and brigade enterprise" in Chinese official documents was replaced with "township and village enterprise."

Table 3 The development of CBEs during the Cultural Revolution

County name		SOE outputs in 1966 (%)	SOE outputs in 1978 (%)	CBE outputs in 1978 (%)
Jiangsu province				
Suzhou	Taicang county	81.97	46.37	40.39
	Zhang Jiagang county	82.72	24.18	63.29
	Wu county	83.87	32.25	50.85
Wuxi	Wuxi county	66.8	20.94	64.85
	Jiangyin county	52.24	30.57	55.34
	Yixing county	68.23	37.87	44.8
Zhejiang province				
Ningbo	Yin county	N.A.	<40	60
	Cixi county	80.28	43.96	51.98
	Yuyao county	68.76	29.5	46.96
	Ninghai county	81.58	39.04	43.15
Wenzhou	Yueqing county	40.21	28.87	42
	Pingyang county	N.A.	<50	41.07
	Yongjia county	56.52	16.78	42.54

during the Cultural Revolution, the Ningbo and Wenzhou regions in Zhejiang province experienced a notable increase in the development of CBEs (see Table 3). Particularly noteworthy was the collective industry in Yin County, which accounted for 60 percent of the total industrial output value of the county in 1978.[32] The collective industries in Cixi, Yuyao, and Ninghai counties also contributed significantly to the respective counties' industrial output value, accounting for 51.98 percent, 46.96 percent, and 43.15 percent of the total, respectively. In contrast, the proportion of state-owned industries in the Ningbo region decreased rapidly during this period. Prior to the Cultural Revolution, most counties in Ningbo had a substantial presence of state-owned industries, accounting for 65 percent to 80 percent of the industrial output. However, by the late 1970s, this percentage had declined to less than 50 percent.[33]

---

[32] Yin County Gazetteer. 1996. Beijing: Zhonghua Publishing House, pp. 619–623.

[33] Cixi County Gazetteer. 1992. Hangzhou: Zhejiang People's Publishing House, p. 385; Yuyao County Gazetteer. 1993. Hangzhou: Zhejiang People's Publishing House, pp. 307–311; Ninghai County Gazetteer. 1993. Hangzhou: Zhejiang People's Publishing House, pp. 350–351.

In a similar fashion, the Wenzhou region experienced a surge in collective industry during the Cultural Revolution. The collective industries in Yueqing, Pingyang, and Yongjia counties contributed over 40 percent of the total industrial output value of their respective counties in 1978. Notably, the proportion of state-owned industries in the Wenzhou region also experienced a sharp decline, with both Yueqing and Yongjia counties having a proportion of less than 30 percent in 1978.[34] After 1978, TVEs flourished as the primary drivers of the regional economy in the Wenzhou region. By the early 1990s, TVEs accounted for over 60 percent of both the total industrial output value and industrial added value, highlighting their vital role in the region's economic growth.[35]

Jiangsu province also witnessed a notable growth in the development of CBEs during the Cultural Revolution. In October 1975, the central government's mouthpiece Red Flag (*hongqi*) magazine published an article titled "A Promising New Development: The Investigation Report on the Development of Commune and Brigades Industry in Wuxi County, Jiangsu Province," which not only affirmed the development of collective enterprise industry but also put an end to the ideological debate on whether peasants could engage in industrial activities.[36] The most rapid development of CBEs in Jiangsu Province was in Wuxi County, where the proportion of collective industrial output value in the total industrial output value of the county reached 64.84 percent by the end of 1978, while the proportion of state-owned industries dropped from 66.8 percent in 1965 to 20.94 percent.[37] Similarly, the collective industries in Jiangyin and Yixing counties in the Wuxi region underwent rapid growth during this period. As shown in Table 3, the collective industrial output value accounted for 55.34 percent and 44.80 percent of the total industrial output value in Jiangyin and Yixing counties, respectively, in 1978. Meanwhile, the proportion of state-owned industries in both counties had markedly decreased since 1966, falling to less than 40 percent by 1978.[38]

---

[34] Yueqing County Gazetteer. 2000. Beijing: People's Publishing House, pp. 505–506; Yongjia County Gazetteer. 2003. Beijing: Fangzhi Chubanshe, pp. 560–561; Pingyang County Gazetteer. 1993. Shanghai: Chinese Dictionary Publishing House, p. 277.

[35] Wenzhou City Gazetteer. 1998. Beijing: Zhonghua Publishing House, p. 1094.

[36] Red Flag (*hongqi*), October 1, 1975. "Dayou Xiwang de Xinsheng Shiwu – Jiangsu Wuxixian Fazhan Shedui Gongye de Diaocha Baogao" (A Promising New Development: The Investigation Report on the Development of Commune and Brigades Industry in Wuxi County, Jiangsu Province).

[37] Wuxi County Gazetteer. 1994. Shanghai: Shanghai Academy of Social Sciences Press, p. 288 and p. 315.

[38] Jiangyin County Gazetteer. 1992. Shanghai: Shanghai People's Publishing House, pp. 337–341; Yixing County Gazetteer. 1990. Shanghai: Shanghai People's Publishing House, pp. 216–217.

The Suzhou region experienced a similar trend during the Cultural Revolution. The collective industry in Zhangjiagang county gradually took shape, accounting for 63.29 percent of the total industrial output value of the county in 1978, while the proportion of state-owned industries had dropped to 28.88 percent in 1976 and further declined to 19.47 percent in 1980.[39] In Taicang county, the collective industry accounted for approximately 40 percent of the total industrial output value of the county in 1978, while the proportion of state-owned industries had decreased to below 50 percent.[40] In Wu county, the collective industry accounted for 50.85 percent of the total industrial output value of the county in 1978, while the proportion of state-owned industries dropped from 83.87 percent in 1966 to 32.25 percent in 1978.[41] In a sense, these regions had undergone a transformation in industrial ownership before 1978, which sowed the seeds for the subsequent development of the private economy. In the 1980s, TVEs, which succeeded CBEs, "suddenly emerged as a new force" (*yijun tuqi*), serving as a major engine for the country's economic expansion.[42]

The surge of collective industries was also a notable feature of the economic transformation in Fujian and Guangdong provinces. To take an example, during the Cultural Revolution, Jinjiang City of Fujian province experienced a substantial increase in the proportion of collective industrial output value in total industrial output, reaching approximately 38.43 percent in 1978. This growth was accompanied by a decline in the proportion of state-owned industries, which had decreased from 55.63 percent in 1965 to 31.67 percent by 1978.[43] The most significant ownership change occurred in Shishi City, previously under the jurisdiction of Jinjiang, where the proportion of state-owned industries in total industrial output plummeted from 74.7 percent in 1965 to 17.6 percent in 1978.[44] Similarly, CBEs in Zengcheng City, Guangdong Province, experienced remarkable development, with the

---

[39] Shazhou County Gazetteer, 1992. Nanjing: Jiangsu People's Publishing House, pp. 365–366.

[40] Taicang County Gazetteer, 1991. Nanjing: Jiangsu People's Publishing House, p. 263.

[41] Wu County Gazetteer, 1994. Shanghai: Shanghai Classics Publishing House, p. 263 and p. 471.

[42] When meeting with Stefan Korosec, a member of the Presidium of the Central Committee of the League of Communists of Yugoslavia in 1987, Deng Xiaoping made a comment on China's rural reform: "In the rural reform our greatest success – and it is one we had by no means anticipated – has been the development of a large number of township and village enterprises. They have engaged in the most diverse endeavours, including both manufacturing and trade. They suddenly emerged as a new force. The Central Committee takes no credit for this" (Deng, 1993, p. 208).

[43] Jinjiang City Gazetteer, 1994. Shanghai: Shanghai Joint Publishing, p. 304.

[44] Shishi City Gazetteer, 1998. Beijing: Fangzhi Chubanshe, p. 286.

proportion of collective industries in total industrial output value reaching 40.41 percentby 1978.[45]

Even in Northeastern China, an area where the state-owned industry was deeply entrenched, CBEs seized the window of opportunity provided by economic decentralization to take root and thrive. For example, in Jilin province, the local "five small" industry also experienced rapid development amidst decentralization. According to statistics, the number of collectively owned industrial enterprises in the province grew from 2,178 in 1969 to 4,343 in 1975, doubling in a span of just six years (Shi, 2008, p. 79). By 1976, the total industrial output value of collectively owned enterprises in Heilongjiang, Jilin, and Liaoning provinces reached 2.453 billion yuan, 2.041 billion yuan, and 6.052 billion yuan respectively, all significantly higher than the figures reported in 1971, with Heilongjiang doubling, Jilin tripling, and Liaoning more than doubling (Shi, 2008, p. 80).

During the Cultural Revolution, economic decentralization facilitated a considerable flow of state resources to CBEs. As it turned out, a substantial proportion of the investment for rural industrialization was financed by state funds: local governments and industrial bureaus utilized decentralized state funds to invest in new enterprises, while also instructing existing state and collective enterprises to provide support to commune enterprises, with the associated costs ultimately borne by the state plan (Wong, 1991). Local officials facilitated access to capital, technology, and distribution channels for certain CBEs, allowing them to benefit from budgetary grants, bank loans, and state economic plans (Whiting, 2000, chapter 2). The rise of local collective enterprises represents a crucial aspect of the "silent revolution," wherein villagers reconnected with market mechanisms through private farming, trading on the black market, establishing local enterprises, and migrating to urban areas for better economic opportunities during the Cultural Revolution (Dikötter, 2016).

Figure 5 demonstrates that after 1970, collective enterprises, the precursors of TVEs, began to contribute a larger share to industrial output. The proportion of collective enterprise output in total industrial output grew from 12.4 percent to 22.4 percent between 1970 and 1978.[46] While CBEs were often labeled as "collective" to align with the state's ideological framework, in practice, many operated largely on private lines (Dikötter, 2016). In fact, the overwhelming majority of TVEs were private enterprises as opposed to collective ones

---

[45] Zengcheng County Gazetteer, 1995. Guangzhou: Guangdong People's Publishing House, p. 320.

[46] Figure 5 also reveals that the boom in collective enterprises financed with local revenue quickly came to an end in the early 1960s as spending authority recentralized.

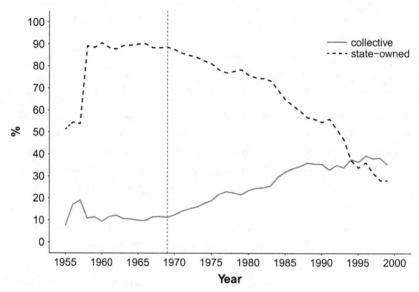

Figure 5 SOE and collective share in industrial output (%).
Source: China Statistical Yearbook (Various Years)

(Huang, 2012). In short, the Cultural Revolution created a moment of economic decentralization which enabled local officials to protect local entrepreneurs against national-level radical policies, thereby fostering the rise of capitalism characterized by vibrant private economic activities in certain regions (Zhang et al., 2021).

Finally, the decentralization of infrastructure investment and materials allocation also began in the early 1970s. Infrastructure construction saw a pilot of a contracting approach where local authorities were tasked with infrastructure development while following specific construction tasks set by the central government. Moreover, local authorities were responsible for overall planning and investment allocation, including equipment and materials, with any surplus materials to be retained at the local level. In parallel with enterprise decentralization, a contracting approach was introduced for material allocation, which involved adjustments to the scope of centrally managed materials and the decentralization of material management authority. In 1972, a pilot program was initiated in Jiangsu and northern China, transferring the material allocation authority of more than 400 SOEs to local authorities. Subsequently, in 1976, provinces such as Shanghai, Hubei, Guangdong, Qinghai, and others assumed the responsibility of materials allocation and supply for 166 SOEs that had been decentralized to local governments (Zhao, 1989, pp. 46–47).

Except for the period of the Great Leap Forward, Figure 6 illustrates that 90 percent of capital construction investment prior to 1970 was directly

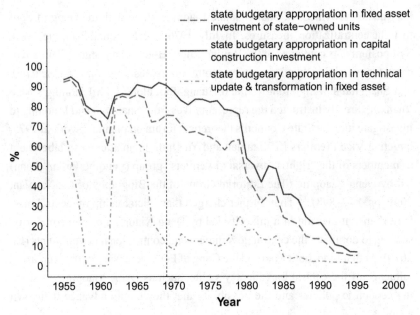

Figure 6 Share of fixed asset, capital construction, and technical update investment financed by budgetary appropriation (%).
Source: China Statistical Yearbook on Fixed Assets Investment (Various Years)

allocated from the central budget. After 1970, however, firms began to tap into increasingly diverse financing channels. Essentially, the transfer of SOE ownership from the central to the local level allowed local governments to establish new firms and make investments with self-raised funds, which operated outside formal budgetary channels (Wong, Heady, and Woo, 1995). As Figure 4 shows, extrabudgetary revenue grew by at least 10 percent per year in the first half of the 1970s. Throughout much of the 1970s, local government construction investment exceeded central investment. Taken together, the extensive evidence presented in the preceding analysis echoes Xu's (2011: p. 1086) observation that "after the end of the Cultural Revolution, subnational governments already de facto controlled a great deal of resources in China."

In the 1970s, the central planners attempted to revive the state-owned economy. Notably, after Deng Xiaoping took office as Vice Premier in January 1975, he took measures to rectify the economy. From June to August, the State Council convened a theoretical forum on planning work (*jihua gongzuo wuxuhui*) to discuss the direction, principles, and policies of economic work. The meeting identified disorder and fragmentation as the primary problems in the economic landscape and stressed the importance of thorough rectification, with a particular emphasis on centralization. However, there is evidence suggesting that the key provinces of Shanghai and Liaoning allied with the Gang of Four to fight centralization measures. In July 1976, the National Planning Work Symposium was convened at the Beijing Jingxi Hotel. The Gang of Four advocated for criticizing "dictatorship by central ministries" (*tiaotiao zhuanzheng*), and Shanghai's Wang Hongwen and Huang Tao, along with Liaoning's Mao Yuanxin, directly instructed the representatives from Shanghai and Liaoning to investigate into the State Council's theoretical forum on planning work in 1975, targeting Vice Premiers Li Xiannian and Yu Qiuli, in an attempt to label them as members of the "rightist reversal of verdicts" group (youqing fan'an jituan) led by Deng Xiaoping (The Editorial Group of the Biography of Li Xiannian, 2009, pp. 897–898).[47] They further charged that "dictatorship by central ministries" meant the rule of a minority led by Deng Xiaoping over the majority, seeking to dominate the central government and control local governments (Li, 2019). At that time, both Mao and the Gang of Four were wary of the increasing influence of the central bureaucracy's elite, such as Deng Xiaoping, in shaping economic policies and the possibility that they would advance their own agendas.

When Deng Xiaoping and Chen Yun ascended to power in the late 1970s, they were confronted with a Central Committee dominated by local officials, many of whom held military leadership positions. This situation remained largely unchanged until the 12th Party Congress in 1982, when the representation of State Council officials in the Central Committee surpassed 30 percent, though still well below historical levels. Unlike Mao, Deng and Chen ruled by coalition building and were unable to completely overhaul the elite selectorate. As shown in Figure 1, even at the height of Deng's campaign to force colleagues into retirement at the 13th Party Congress, the incumbency ratio in the Central Committee remained above 45 percent, approximately 15 percent higher than at the Ninth Party Congress. Into the 1990s, the Central Committee incumbency ratio hovered around 70 percent. This demonstrates the stickiness of the elite selectorate, which proved resistant to radical transformations within a short period. In the absence of a wholesale purge like the Cultural Revolution, it took a decade or more to fundamentally reshape the composition of the elite selectorate, thereby providing some medium-term credibility to the preferred policies supported by the elite.

The heavy weight of local leaders in the political elite continued to exert influence on decision making even after the Cultural Revolution. Deng Xiaoping, in his landmark speech of December 13, 1978, "Emancipate the Mind, Seek Truth from Facts and Unite as One in Looking to the Future" (*jiefang sixiang,*

---

[47] Beginning in late 1975, Deng faced criticism for his "rightist reversal of verdicts," which had allowed too many senior officials to return to work.

shishiqiushi, tuanjie yizhi xiangqiankan), highlighted the importance of local autonomy in boosting economic growth:

> At present, our country's economic management system is excessively centralized. There should be a planned and courageous decentralization, as otherwise it will not be conducive to fully harnessing the initiative from the four aspects of state, localities, enterprises, and individual workers, nor will it be conducive to implementing modern economic management and improving labor productivity. We should give local governments, enterprises, and production teams more autonomy in operation and management (Deng, 1994, p. 145).

Of course, there have always been demands from the central elite for enhancing control over local financial authority. For example, at the Central Working Conference in 1980, Chen Yun proposed that:

> In the coming years, both the central and local governments should greatly tighten their spending. Local government surpluses will be borrowed by the central government, but financial power still belongs to the local governments. Local government surpluses must be frozen, otherwise local governments will invest and spend recklessly, and the central government will not be able to balance the budget ... All government agencies, organizations, military units, enterprises, and public institutions must not use their surplus from the previous year. If it is imperative to use them, approval must be obtained. This approach is centralization. A country like ours cannot function without such centralization, otherwise we will be in chaos and it will not be conducive to reform (Chen, 2011b, pp. 525–526).

Nevertheless, in February 1980, the State Council implemented a crucial fiscal system reform, adopting the "Dividing Revenue and Expenditure, Contracting by Different Administrative Levels" (*huafen shouzhi, fenji baogan*) system, also known as the "Eating in Separate Kitchens" (*fenzao chifan*) system. Under this fiscal system, the central government clearly delineated the scope of fiscal revenue and expenditure with provincial governments, determined a contracting base with each province, and set the proportions of remittance and retention based on the contracting base. Local governments typically enjoyed high revenue-retention rates. Within this defined scope, local governments had the authority to manage their own revenue and expenditure to achieve fiscal balance. This fiscal system significantly expanded the fiscal autonomy of local governments and motivated local governments to expand their tax bases by promoting economic development.[48] From 1985 to 1988, the

---

[48] During this period, Guangdong and Fujian implemented a special "Big Contracting" (*da baogan*) system that adopted fixed remittance and subsidies rather than proportional ones. Guangdong practiced fixed remittance, while Fujian, with revenue lower than expenditures,

central government implemented "Dividing Tax Types, Binding Revenue and Expenditure, Contracting by Administrative Levels" (*huafen shuizhong, heding shouzhi, fenji baogan*). Provincial and local governments still retained high levels of fiscal autonomy.[49]

The debates in the development of TVEs also demonstrate the same logic. During the late 1970s to the early 1980s, as the central government assumed control and undertook economic restructuring, there were voices within the central government advocating for the centralization of economic authority. For instance, in a Politburo meeting in March 1979, Chen Yun suggested that:

> Currently, there are numerous industrial enterprises run by communes, as well as small-scale township industries. There are valid reasons for establishing these industries, with the primary aim to create employment opportunities and improve living standards. However, there is also a degree of blindness in this endeavor . . . If local and commune-run industries compete with large-scale industries for raw materials and electricity, they should be phased out (Chen, 2011a, pp. 67–71).

In November 1980, at the National Planning Conference convened by the State Council, some ministries proposed that CBEs should be prohibited from operating in a dozen or so major industries. In December 1980, the Party center convened a work conference to assess the economic situation and resolved to further adjust the national economy starting from 1981 onwards. In January 1981, at the executive meeting of the State Council, when discussing the closure and transformation of some small CBEs, Premier Zhao Ziyang opposed harsh policies toward CBEs and said: "Do not shut them down hastily. As long as

---

applied fixed subsidies. Under this system, any additional revenue beyond the contracting base belonged solely to the local government, with the central government no longer sharing in the excess. Meanwhile, Jiangsu continued to use the "Fixed Ratio Contracting" (*guding bili baogan*) system, while Beijing, Tianjin, and Shanghai adopted the "Sharing Total Revenue, Setting Once a Year" (*zong'e fencheng, yinian yiding*) system. Finally, ethnic autonomous regions, also including Qinghai, Yunnan, and Guizhou provinces, implemented a "Dividing Revenue and Expenditure, Contracting by Different Administrative Levels (*huafen shouzhi, fenji baogan*)" system, with policies more favorable to their needs. For a detailed discussion, see Liu and Jia (2008, p. 31).

[49] After the tax-for-profit reform, revenue was divided by tax types between the central and local governments. The revenue was categorized into three types: central fiscal revenue, local fiscal revenue, and shared revenue between the central and local governments. Meanwhile, expenditures were allocated by administrative levels. Central expenditures primarily comprised central infrastructure investment, defense, diplomacy, and expenditures for education, science, culture, and health at the central level. Local fiscal expenditures mainly included local economic construction expenditures, as well as expenditures for education, science, culture, and health at the local level. For a detailed discussion, see Liu and Jia (2008, pp. 34–35).

they can produce, their goods have a market, and they can sustain themselves, let them continue to operate; do not shut them down or stop them" (Ma, 1991, p. 91). Nevertheless, from 1981 to 1983, the development of CBEs slowed down during the economic readjustment.

The year 1984 marked a pivotal moment in the development of TVEs in China. In January 1984, the Ministry of Agriculture, Animal Husbandry, and Fishery held a national conference in Beijing, focusing on the policies toward CBEs. The conference centered on a report on CBEs, which was the culmination of over two years of intensive research following General Secretary Hu Yaobang's directives. The report recognized that CBEs had emerged as a vital force in China's national economy.[50] In March 1984, the CCP's Central Committee and the State Council officially disseminated the amended report as an official document. This document not only renamed CBEs as TVEs, but also actively encouraged local governments to foster their development, provide necessary support, and accord them equal treatment with state-owned enterprises (Ma, 1991, pp. 107–110). Subsequent to this official recognition, there was an astonishing 355 percent increase in the number of TVEs, a 61 percent rise in the total number of employees, and a 68 percent growth in output value in 1984 (Pan, 2003, p. 98). Overall, the year 1984 witnessed the official approval and rapid development of TVEs, solidifying their indispensable role in China's economy.

Although Deng Xiaoping, along with Liu Shaoqi, had centralized the fiscal system in the early 1960s, as the supreme leader of China, he could not afford to directly offend the majority in the Central Committee. Even a staunch supporter of central planning like Chen Yun supported provincial fiscal contracts over the Ministry of Finance's objection, as he faced the same political constituency (Deng, 2005, p. 144). The provincial majority in the CC at the time had the muscle to force a showdown (*tanpai*) with Deng and Chen (Shirk, 1993, 165). In 1986, the State Council's plan to replace the tax-contracting system with a more centralized tax-sharing system faced pushback from local officials (Zhang, 2007). The report from the 13th Party Congress in 1987 further implied that a potential direction for future economic reforms entailed "implementing a

---

[50] It is also worth noting that the CCP's Document NO.1 of 1983 clearly suggested that "the existing CBEs not only serve as economic entities that support agricultural production, but also provide services for the various economic activities of farmers. They should be carefully protected during the process of institutional reform, ensuring that they are not weakened and preventing any arbitrary destruction or dismantling." See, "Notice of the Central Committee of the CCP on Issuing 'Several Issues Regarding Current Rural Economic Policies' (*Zhonggong Zhongyang Guanyu Yinfa Dangqian Nongcun Jingji Zhengce de Ruogan Wenti de Tongzhi*)."

tax-sharing system based on a reasonable delineation of central and local fiscal revenues and expenditures, and properly manage the economic interests among the central and local governments, state, enterprises, and individuals."[51]

In July 1988, the State Council of China issued a document titled "Decision on the Implementation of Fiscal Contracting at the Local Level," which built upon the fiscal contracting system of the 1980s and incorporated the cities specifically designated in the state plan (*jihua danlie shi*) into the scope of fiscal contracting. This document stipulated six different forms of fiscal contracting methods to thirty-seven provincial-level administrative units across the country. This fiscal system was also known as "Big Contracting" (*da baogan*).[52] The document emphasized: "Once the fiscal contracting method is established, each region should strive to develop the economy, tap potential resources, explore revenue sources, increase income, and strengthen local fiscal capacity in line with national policies and plan requirements ... Each region should seriously implement the contracting method and take responsibility for any surpluses or deficits."[53]

To be sure, the continuation of decentralized fiscal system in the 1980s was sustained by political incentives. Conservative leaders at the central government such as Li Peng were reluctant to antagonize provincial leaders by imposing policies to roll back economic decentralization in the sense that "the influence of provincial officials with the CCP had grown to the point that no contender to top leadership stood a chance of winning without the support of at least some provincial officials" (Shirk, 1993, p. 194). After the purge of Zhao Ziyang after the Tiananmen crackdown, conservative leaders, such as Yao Yilin, proposed to centralize fiscal authority but encountered strong resistance from provincial leaders (Shirk, 1993, p. 194). In particular, Ye Xuanping,

---

[51] Zhao Ziyang. "Advancing along the Road of Socialism with Chinese Characteristics – Report at the 13th National Congress of the Chinese Communist Party." October 25, 1987. www.gov .cn/test/2007-08/29/content_730445.htm.

[52] For example, ten provinces and cities, including Beijing, Hebei, and Jiangsu, implemented the "Incremental Revenue Contracting" (*shouru dizeng baogan*) method. Based on each region's 1987 final revenue and expenditure and most recent revenue growth, the central government determined local revenue growth rates, revenue retention ratios, and remittance ratios. For revenue within the growth target, the central and local governments shared revenue proportionately. Revenue in excess of the growth target was retained entirely by the local government. If a region's revenue failed to reach the growth target, the local government utilized its own funds to finance the remittance amount owed to the central government. Sixteen provinces and cities, including Jilin, Jiangxi, and Shaanxi, adopted a "Fixed Subsidy Contracting" (*ding'e buzhu*) fiscal system. Based on previously approved revenue and expenditure baselines, the central government provided fixed subsidies for the portion where expenditure exceeded revenue.

[53] Guowuyuan Guanyu Difang Shixing Caizheng Baogan Banfa de Jueding (Decision on the Implementation of Fiscal Contracting at the Local Level). July 28, 1988. www.gov.cn/xxgk/ pub/govpublic/mrlm/201110/t20111010_64119.html (accessed on September 12, 2023).

the governor of Guangdong province and the son of Marshal Ye Jianying, played a leading role in safeguarding financial autonomy and resisting to the central government's centralization proposals (Montinola, Qian, and Weingast, 1995; Qian and Weingast, 1997). During several meetings during 1989–1990, Ye criticized centralization plans. His speeches were well received by other provincial leaders and were reportedly met with "wild applause" at a conference (Cai and Treisman, 2006).

Despite the growing influence of elites at the State Council during the 1980s, their political clout still had yet to prevail in the Central Committee relative to that of local officials. As a result, the implementation of centralization policies would face substantial political resistance, thereby creating a relatively stable environment for economic decentralization. For instance, between 1982 and 1992, the fiscal contracting system held a fair degree of credibility, as evidenced by the negligible discrepancy between the contractual revenue retention amount stipulated in the ex ante fiscal contracts and the actual provincial expenditure (Jin, Qian, and Weingast, 2005).[54]

Not surprisingly, with the exception of some retrenchment in fiscal revenue, most of our indicators illustrate that decentralization policies remained in effect throughout much of the 1980s, reinforcing the general observation of substantial local fiscal autonomy during that period (Montinola, Qian, and Weingast, 1995; Oi, 1992; Wong, Heady, and Woo, 1995). Unlike the early 1960s, rapid recentralization was not a politically viable alternative.

3.5 Regaining the commanding heights: The rise of technocrats in the 1990s and beyond

The reform era in China witnessed a gradual increase in the presence of central officials in the Central Committee, which culminated in their reassertion of dominance in the Central Committee during the 1990s. Following the Cultural Revolution, Chen Yun, a crucial ally of Deng Xiaoping in the struggle against Hua Guofeng, endeavored to rebuild the various ministries and offices in the State Council, which had historically served as his traditional power base prior to the Cultural Revolution (Cui, 2003; Shih, 2008).

In the 1980s, with the rapid growth and increasing complexity of the Chinese economy, the central government recognized a need for additional regulatory agencies to address emerging challenges, such as information asymmetry, inflation, corruption, and trade friction (Fan, Hai, and Woo, 1996; Fewsmith, 2016).

---

[54] Wong (1992) provides evidence that when facing the decline of revenues, central government repeatedly tampered with revenue-sharing schemes.

In response to these issues, a number of ministerial or vice-ministerial level agencies, including the Export-Import Commission, the Special Economic Zone Office, the State Economic Commission, the State Statistical Bureau, and the four specialized banks, were established within the central government. Given the administrative rank of these entities, their leaders were granted either full or alternate membership in the Central Committee.

The rise of technocrats also aligned with Deng's efforts to rejuvenate the leadership (Cui, 2003). A key component of Deng's rejuvenation campaign was the systematic transfer of military CC members, many of whom held provincial positions, to the Central Advisory Committee or to full retirement, while younger, more educated officials were placed in new State Council positions (Manion, 1993). At the same time, the Organization Department began to consider CEOs of large state-owned enterprises as potential candidates for the Central Committee (Cui, 2003, p. 94). These various forces contributed to a steady increase in the proportion of State Council officials within the Central Committee throughout the 1980s and early 1990s. Consequently, the number of State Council CC members surpassed that of provincial members by the 14th Party Congress in 1992, as shown in Figure 3.

As a result of the gradual consolidation of power by central officials during the 1980s, the top leaders who advanced centralization policies in the 1990s enjoyed the backing of a considerable bloc of central officials within the Central Committee. To be sure, the shift from the tax-contracting to the tax-sharing system, a milestone in fiscal centralization, required tremendous political will from the central leadership and the dismissal of a few recalcitrant provincial leaders (Brahm, 2002; Fewsmith, 2001; Yang, 1997, 2004).

With respect to the tax-sharing system, affluent coastal provinces often regarded it as a means of "robbing the rich to help the poor" (*jiefu jipin*), and some leaders from these provinces reportedly aimed to thwart the central government's endeavors to reassert its fiscal authority (Chung, 1994). The Party's top leadership wielded their personnel power to undermine local resistance. Notably, in 1991, two of Guangdong's most senior officials, the Party Secretary Lin Ruo and Governor Ye Xuanping, both aged 67, experienced a change in their official roles. Lin Ruo became the Chairman of the Guangdong Provincial People's Congress, while Ye Xuanping was "promoted" to a ceremonial position as Vice Chairman of the Chinese People's Political Consultative Conference (CPPCC). Xie Fei and Zhu Senlin, two younger and less powerful leaders, succeeded as the Party Secretary and Provincial Governor, respectively, following the changes in leadership. In the case of Jiangsu province, the "fiery" arguments between Vice Premier Zhu Rongji and provincial leaders over tax reforms ultimately resulted in the removal of Jiangsu's Party

Secretary Shen Daren in late 1993.[55] In addition, to enhance the Party's control over Zhejiang province, Li Zemin was "parachuted" from Liaoning province to serve as the Party Secretary in Zhejiang province in 1988. Ge Hongsheng, who rose through the ranks in Zhejiang and served as its governor, was dismissed during the 1993 leadership reshuffle, possibly as a result of his vocal opposition to the tax-sharing system (Kim, 2004). Because both Jiang Zemin and Zhu Rongji came from Shanghai, the leaders in Shanghai expressed some concerns over the specific policies but in general supported the Party center's tax reform proposals.

From September to November 1993, Zhu Rongji, then Executive Vice Premier of the State Council, visited seventeen provinces and autonomous regions with leaders from the Ministry of Finance and other ministries to listen to the views of local governments, in effect bargaining with them over the implementation of the tax-sharing system (Liu and Jia, 2008, p. 351). According to the recollections of the participants at that time, the resistance from Guangdong province was the greatest. The leaders of Guangdong hoped to maintain the fiscal contracting system. In Zhu Rongji's words, despite the fact that the Party Secretary Xie Fei and Governor Zhu Senlin in Guangdong province "spoke up strongly for Guangdong's interests," in the end they "embodied Guangdong's spirit and stance on keeping the big picture in mind and upholding the interests of the nation" (Zhu, 2013, p. 178). Although the proposal of the tax-sharing system met with varying degrees of resistance in other parts of the country, it was accepted by local governments across the country in a matter of months under pressure from the central government.

The tax-sharing system reform was eventually implemented as a means of centralizing fiscal control. This reform involved the clear categorization of central taxes, local taxes, and shared taxes. Under the new system, the value-added tax, a major source of local fiscal revenues, became a shared tax, with 75 percent of the revenue directed to the central government and the remaining 25 percent allocated to local governments (Xiang, 2006, p. 153). As part of the tax-sharing reform, organizational restructuring was undertaken, which involved the establishment of national tax bureaus (*guo shui ju*) and local tax bureaus (*di shui ju*). This restructuring entailed placing all tax bureaus under the direct supervision of the State Administration of Taxation, effectively reasserting vertical (*tiao-tiao*) control over the horizontal (*kuaikuai*) management of tax collection and administration. Specifically, local tax bureaus were tasked with collecting local taxes, while national tax bureaus were responsible for collecting central taxes. However, it is important to note that all shared taxes were first sent to national

---

[55] South China Morning Post, December 8, 1993. "Strange Case of the Missing Economic Czar."

tax offices, which then distributed them to local governments in accordance with a predetermined ratio.

In addition, on an annual basis, the central government provided a large amount of fiscal transfers to local governments to address their spending gaps. These transfers reflected the central government's preferences regarding expenditure responsibilities and had a considerable impact on the fiscal autonomy of local governments, particularly in the case of earmarked transfers. Local governments were required to adhere strictly to the designated purposes of these funds and were subject to audit by the central government.[56] In brief, the tax-sharing reform centralized a considerable proportion of tax revenues to the central government, strengthening its capacity for taxation and its authority in assigning expenditure responsibilities to local governments.

By the early 1990s, local officials were no longer in the position to force a showdown with central leaders. By that time, State Council and central SOE officials constituted more than 30 percent of the CC, while central officials as a whole formed nearly the majority following the 1992 14th Party Congress, as shown in Figures 2 and 3. The dominating presence of provincial officials in the CC began to wane in the late 1980s and further slipped at the 14th Party Congress in 1992.

Given this new political alignment, Huang's (2008) excellent study and our indicators reveal a pattern of centralization of the Chinese economy in the 1990s and beyond. Huang (2008) provides evidence that many of the successful policies implemented in the 1980s, including fiscal decentralization and private-sector financing, experienced a reversal in the 1990s. Figure 4 illustrates the widely recognized decline in the local share of revenue following the tax-sharing reform in 1994, along with a dramatic fall in extrabudgetary revenue relative to the national budget.

Despite China's departure from centrally planned economy and its embrace of more market-oriented reforms in the early stages of economic reform (Naughton, 1996), political leaders reconstructed the state sector and prioritized urban SOEs in the 1990s, leading to the subsequent rise of a powerful state sector in the 2000s (Eaton, 2016; Huang, 2008). In the 1990s, the Chinese government opted to retain control of SOEs in "commanding heights" industries, reshaping the SOE sector by enacting the "grasping the big, letting go of the small" policy, which entailed privatizing small and medium-sized

---

[56] Despite the centralization of the fiscal system after 1994, it was not implemented to the same extent as in the pre–Cultural Revolution period. Notably, the expenditures at subnational levels accounted for approximately 70 percent of all government spending (Landry, 2008). Our analysis focuses more on fiscal revenues rather than expenditures because fiscal transfers from the Ministry of Finance in Beijing financed much of the local expenditure.

SOEs while consolidating control over large SOEs in strategic industries (Eaton, 2016). In parallel, the central government pursued the corporatization and merger of SOEs into large conglomerates, facilitating their listing on both domestic and international stock markets (Walter and Howie, 2011). In 2003, the establishment of the State-Owned Assets Supervision and Administration Commission (SASAC) placed large SOE business groups under ownership control (Naughton, 2015).

In part as a result of the consolidation of the SOE sector, the performance of Chinese SOEs experienced marked improvement in the 2000s. Between 2003 and 2011, the total SOE assets soared from RMB 19.71 trillion to RMB 85.37 trillion, amounting to a 20.1 percent annual growth rate, while the total profits surged substantially from RMB 0.50 trillion to RMB 2.58 trillion over the same period, reflecting a 22.9 percent annual increase (SASAC Yearbooks, 2004 and 2012). The SOE sector exhibited a trend toward centralization of economic resources. The total assets of central SOEs, representing approximately 21,000 or 18.1 percent of all SOEs in 2006, increased from 38.9 percent of all SOE assets in 1997 to 51.7 percent in 2006, while concurrently contributing 51.2 percent of the total SOE revenues and 64.0 percent of the total SOE profits (OECD, 2009). With large SOEs playing an increasingly important role in China's domestic and international economic and political landscape, both academics and policy circles have characterized China's economic model as state capitalism (e.g., Bremmer, 2010; Eaton, 2016; Lin and Milhaupt, 2013; Naughton and Tsai, 2015).

Under both Hu Jintao and Xi Jinping, the goal was to establish SOEs that are both competitive in the market and obedient to the Party. Xi, rather than deviating from the past, intensified and formalized established practices, shifting more toward Party-led control mechanisms as opposed to Hu's reliance on the state bureaucracy, particularly the SASAC (Leutert and Eaton, 2021). Nevertheless, since Xi Jinping assumed leadership in 2012, the SOE sector has become even more deeply entrenched. The CCP's prioritization of regime security has led to efforts aimed at enhancing Party control over the economy (Pearson, Rithmire, and Tsai, 2022, 2023). In the course of his speeches at the 19th Party Congress in late 2017, and later at the National People's Congress in early 2018, Xi advocated for an expanded role of the Party, notably strengthening the role of Party committees, even in the private sector.

More critical for China's current investment-dependent economic model, the central government has dramatically centralized investment funding sources, including budgetary allocations, major state bank loans, and bond and stock issuance approved by central agencies. Figure 6 shows that for a while, central budgetary allocation was replaced by local extrabudgetary income and increasingly bank loans. However, the 1990s saw loans from centrally controlled state banks becoming a major source of funding for investment (Shih, 2008).

Alongside the consolidation of SOEs and the rising share of central officials in the Central Committee, from 2012 to 2015, the pace of private investment slowed markedly, and in 2016, it fell below that of state investment (Lardy, 2019). The share of investment undertaken by either the central government or SOEs bottomed out in the early 2010s and actually began to rise in 2015 (Lardy, 2019). The centralization of economic resources, facilitated by the accumulation of central political clout, has perpetuated the dominance of the central government in China's investment-led growth model.

4 Taiwan

The association between the composition of the party elite and policy orientations is not unique to mainland China but also applies to other Leninist regimes, including Taiwan under the authoritarian rule of the Kuomintang (KMT). Although the causal link between changing elite composition and policy orientations in these cases may not be as stark as in China, they do suggest that elite composition played a role, at least in facilitating the implementation of new policies without significant reversals. In this section, we use Taiwan as a shadow case to illustrate this point.

4.1 Rebuilding the Party-State in Taiwan

During its rule in mainland China, the Kuomintang (KMT) was plagued by internal factional conflicts and a lack of discipline. The KMT's ruling coalition comprised of a diverse range of interests, including former warlords who demanded considerable autonomy and resisted the efforts to consolidate central control and curb corruption (Wang, 2003).

In the Chinese Civil War, the KMT was ultimately defeated by the CCP and was compelled to retreat to Taiwan in 1949. The KMT's defeat in the Civil War was a profoundly traumatic experience for Chiang Kai-shek. In January 1949, Chiang attributed the imminent defeat to "the paralysis of the party" and believed that "the membership, organizational structure, and method of leadership all created problems" (Eastman, 1984, pp. 207–208). Upon further reflection, he concluded that the CCP's triumph was due to its superior organizational power, whereas the KMT was unable to ensure compliance from the central government, military, and local authorities (Dickson, 1993). In Taiwan, Chiang was determined to revitalize the KMT, with the hope of retaking the Chinese mainland from the CCP.

In 1950, Chiang established the Central Reform Committee (*zhongyang gaizao weiyuanhui*) to replace the Party's two most powerful agencies on the mainland, namely the Central Standing Committee and the Central Executive Committee. Importantly, Chiang appointed sixteen hand-picked loyalists to this new organization, while deliberately excluding influential figures in the KMT, such as Chen Guofu and Chen Lifu. In 1947, upon the incorporation of the Three People's Principles Youth League into the KMT, the Party consisted of 286 Central Committee (CC) members and 105 alternate CC members. However, following Chiang Kai-shek's reorganization campaign, the KMT's Seventh Party Congress in 1952 saw a significant downsize to just thirty-three CC members and sixteen alternate CC members. This restructuring effectively curtailed Party factionalism, allowing Chiang to further consolidate his hold on power.

In addition, the KMT endeavored to expand its support base and extend its reach into Taiwan's grassroots communities. To that end, Party branches and cells were established throughout the island in rural villages, government organs, schools, and enterprises. In effect, the KMT built an extensive network of Party cells and committees to monitor the functions of governmental and legislative entities at every level (Dickson, 1993). By the end of 1952, the number of Party members had increased to 170,000, who were organized into 30,000 Party cells (Tien, 1989, p. 67). Moreover, Chiang appointed his son, Chiang Ching-kuo, to lead the General Political Work Department. Chiang Ching-kuo reinstated the political commissar system, which enabled the KMT to establish Party cells within the military and enforce Party discipline among soldiers. As of 1954, 210,000 out of 600,000 members of the armed forces, or 35 percent of the total, were registered Party members (Tien, 1989, p. 68).

The KMT's rural state-building efforts centered on land reforms, which were implemented through a series of new laws enacted between 1949 and 1953. First, the 37.5 percent Arable Rent Reduction Act was passed, stipulating that landlords could not charge rent exceeding 37.5 percent of the land's total annual yield. Subsequently, public land was sold to tenant farmers at prices well below market price. The culmination of these land reforms was the Land-to-the-Tiller program initiated in 1953. Under the Land-to-the-Tiller Act, landowners were required to sell all tenanted land exceeding three hectares to the state, which then resold the land to the tenants (Kay, 2002).[57] As a result,

---

[57] The KMT offered two types of compensation to landlords. 70 percent of the compensation was provided in the form of government-issued bonds, while the remaining 30 percent was in the form of shares in four major state-owned enterprises, namely the Taiwan Cement Corporation, the Paper and Pulp Corporation, the Agriculture and Forestry Development Corporation, and the Industrial and Mining Corporation (Strauss, 2019).

land ownership was effectively transferred from landlords to tenant farmers. Overall, land reforms played a crucial role in the party-state building process by weakening the indigenous Taiwanese landowning elite and social organizations (Albertus, Fenner, and Slater, 2018; Strauss, 2019). These reforms also facilitated the penetration of the party-state into the grassroots of rural society and reshaped rural institutions to align with the dominant party-state's desired image (Strauss, 2019, p. 214).

4.2 An Overview of Taiwan's Economic Liberalization

During the 1950s, Taiwan adopted an import substitution industrialization (ISI) strategy as a means to recover and promote economic development. This involved the implementation of government-imposed restrictive measures to regulate the import of specific foreign industrial goods. The goal was to promote domestic production and enable Taiwan's industrial products to replace foreign materials in the local market. Throughout this period, economic policies were characterized by extensive government controls.

Under ISI model, Taiwan's government imposed high tariffs on a wide range of imported goods to protect domestic industries and drive economic growth. High tariff rates and import controls were applied to shield sectors such as textiles, flour, sugar, plywood, plastics, cement, and paper, which the government was keen to promote. Additionally, to conserve foreign exchange, import restrictions and high tariffs were imposed on luxury goods. In 1955, for instance, the average tariff burden – the ratio of total tariff revenue to the pretariff value of imported goods – reached 30 percent, with certain commodities, such as cotton cloth, subjected to a tariff as high as 40 percent (see Kuo and Myers, 2012, p. 74). Importable goods were subject to three types of controls: prohibited goods that could not be imported by private entities; controlled goods that could be imported but only under strict regulations; and restricted goods that required approval from government entities or imposed restrictions on importers and countries of origin.

In June 1949, Taiwan's government implemented strict foreign exchange regulations, including the Exchange Settlement Certificate (ESC) regime and a fixed exchange rate. Under this system, all export proceeds had to be sold to the Central Bank of China (CBC), with 20 percent sold at the official exchange rate of 5:1 and ESCs issued for the remaining 80 percent for future export or import transactions (Li, 1993a, pp. 49–50). The overvaluation of the New Taiwan dollar spurred import demands. In 1951, a complex multiple exchange rate system was introduced, applying different rates to various exports and imports. Before the exchange rate reform in 1959, more than ten distinct rates were in place, reflecting the government's varying demand for different types of imported commodities. The goal of this system was to curtail unnecessary imports, encourage the import of essential raw materials and machinery, and boost the export of agricultural products.

Deeply influenced by Sun Yat-sen's philosophy of "developing state capital and restraining private capital" (*fada guojia ziben, jiezhi siren ziben*), the KMT elites played a crucial role in shaping Taiwan's economy in the 1950s. One salient feature of Taiwan's economy in the 1950s was the government's substantial control over the economy. The state economy was concentrated in finance, infrastructure, monopolistic businesses, and upstream industries. The establishment of the state sector drew upon several sources, including confiscated Japanese-owned enterprises, state-owned enterprises relocated from mainland China to Taiwan, and the newly established state-owned enterprises in Taiwan. During that period, the public sector's acquisition of large Japanese investments constituted approximately two-thirds of the total industrial capital, while the private sector received approximately a quarter of the capital through small and medium-sized Japanese investments (Chu, 2017, p. 343). As the Civil War between the KMT and the CCP escalated and turned increasingly against the KMT from 1948, the KMT government began transferring a substantial amount of assets to Taiwan, which involved public enterprises. These transferred public enterprises ranged from finance, banking, textiles, steel, synthetic chemicals, coal, machinery, and fishing, to defense industries. Under the government's protection, public enterprises managed to monopolize vital upstream industries in Taiwan, extracting resources from midstream and downstream private enterprises, thereby maintaining their advantageous position in the economic system (Wu, 1992, p. 99). While the private sector witnessed modest growth from 1952 to 1958, the dominance of public enterprises over private enterprises persisted.

In the late 1950s and early 1960s, Taiwan began to ease its economic controls and develop policies for economic liberalization. In terms of the exchange rate system, Taiwan undertook continuous reforms from 1958 to simplify the exchange rate system. The Executive Yuan issued the "Foreign Exchange Trade Reform Plan" (*waihui maoyi gaige fang'an*) and the "Measures for Managing Foreign Exchange and Trade" (*waihui maoyi guanli banfa*), transforming the complex multiple exchange rate system into a dual exchange rate system. This was in preparation for the eventual adoption of a single exchange rate system and involved a substantial devaluation of the New Taiwan Dollar. In 1963, Taiwan officially announced the abolition of the Exchange Settlement Certificate and established a single exchange rate system. In 1956, 51 percent of industrial goods were subject to some form of import controls. By 1961, due to

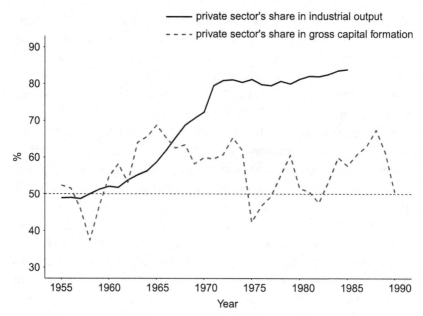

Figure 7 Private sector's share in industrial output and gross capital investment.

Source: Wang (1987) and Wu (1992).

significant alterations to import controls, the proportion of items not subject to import controls increased to 53.7 percent, while prohibited items sharply fell to 3.5 percent (Li, 1993a, p. 27). In 1960, Taiwan enacted the "19-Point Program for Economic and Financial Reform" (*Shijiudian caijing gaige cuoshi*), which encouraged savings and frugal consumption, established a capital market, improved the private investment environment, and supported private industry. In the same year, the "Statute for Encouraging Investment" (*jinagli touzi tiaoli*) was enacted, which provided tax reductions and exemptions to stimulate savings, investments, and exports, and streamlined the administrative procedures to strengthen the acquisition of industrial land. These measures facilitated Taiwan's shift from import substitution to export-oriented economic liberalization.

As a result of these reforms, Taiwan's private economy blossomed. In 1959, the output value of the private industry exceeded 50 percent of the total industrial output. As illustrated in Figure 7, after 1962, private industry grew rapidly, breaking through 60 percent and 70 percent of the total industrial output in 1966 and 1969, respectively, and even exceeding 80 percent in 1972. From 1962 to 1973, private industry exhibited higher growth rates than state-owned or public industry, leading to a rapid transformation of Taiwan's industrial production landscape. From 1952 to 1988, in terms of the gross formation of capital in

Taiwan, private enterprises made a significant contribution during the export expansion period from 1963 to 1972. As Figure 7 shows, the average contribution of private enterprises to the formation of capital in Taiwan increased from 53 percent in 1962 to 64 percent in 1963, reaching approximately 69 percent in 1965. Despite subsequent declines or fluctuations, the overall contribution rate of private enterprises during this period remained at 63 percent, higher than the 49 percent in the import substitution period.

In the 1980s, Taiwan pushed forward a new wave of economic liberalization. In 1984, when Yu Kuo-Hwa became the Premier of the Executive Yuan, he proposed a policy of "liberalization, internationalization, and institutionalization," which set the stage for Taiwan to further open its economy to the outside world. In the 1980s, Taiwan implemented a series of economic liberalization policies, which included the abolishing of interest rate controls and easing foreign exchange restrictions; attracting more foreign investments and further relaxing restrictions on foreign investments; promoting the privatization of state-owned enterprises to improve management efficiency; and further reducing tariffs and easing import controls to promote trade liberalization. These policy changes made Taiwan's economy more open and market-oriented, thus laying a solid foundation for its continuous economic growth and transformation.

4.3 Elite Politics and the Weak Coalition of Technocrats

Following the KMT's retreat to Taiwan, Chiang Kai-shek successfully asserted his authority over other once powerful factions and influential individuals. Notably, warlords like Bai Chongxi and Yan Xishan, weakened by their substantial troop losses in the Chinese Civil War, found their authority in Taiwan significantly eroded. Meanwhile, the CC clique, once a dominant faction within the Nationalist government, saw its influence wane with Chen Guofu's deteriorating health and Chen Lifu's migration to the United States during the early 1950s. Nevertheless, Chiang Kai-shek remained concerned about potential challenges and continued to sideline his rivals within the ruling elite. In a sense, the power struggles within the KMT between 1949 and the mid-1970s can be viewed as the Chiang family's persistent pursuit of "excluding and defeating its rivals in order to establish Chiang Ching-kuo as his father's heir" (Wu, 2005, p. 74). In this endeavor, Chiang Kai-shek strategically positioned his son in key roles within the military, party, and security apparatus, enabling him to amass a broad range of experiences and cultivate extensive political networks.[58]

---

[58] For instance, Ching-kuo had held positions in the General Political Warfare Department, the Political Action Committee, the Party Reform Commission, and the China Youth Corps.

Wu Kuo-chen, previously Chiang Kai-shek's political secretary and the governor of Taiwan since its handover in 1949, encountered disagreements with both Chiang Kai-shek and his son over multiple issues, resulting in his removal from office in 1953. Fearing for his own safety, Wu Kuo-chen hastily fled to the United States after detecting a planned assassination attempt against him (Wu, 1962). To neutralize potential challengers within the military, Chiang Kai-shek reassigned Sun Li-jen, the then commander in chief of the Republic of China Army, to a largely ceremonial role as his chief military adviser in 1954. Furthermore, General Sun was accused of plotting a military coup to overthrow Chiang's rule and was subsequently placed under house arrest in 1955 (Wang, 2007). In the aftermath, as many as 300 officers implicated in the alleged plot were investigated and imprisoned.

In the period before the KMT's retreat to Taiwan, the economic and financial domains were largely under the control of Soong Tse-vung, the brother of Madame Chiang Kai-shek, and her brother-in-law, Kung Hsiang-hsi, both of whom relocated to the United States in the late 1940s. In Taiwan, a group of technocrats, previously working under the leadership of Soong Tse-vun and Kung Hsiang-hsi, came to prominence. They maintained strong ties to Madame Chiang and were collectively referred to as the "presidential residence faction" (or *guandi pai*) (Wu, 2005). Notable figures in this faction included Yu Hung-chun and Hsu P. Y. Having previously served as the mayor of Shanghai and Minister of Finance in mainland China, Yu took on the positions of Governor of the Central Bank and Chairman of the Taiwan Provincial Government in Taiwan. Between 1954 and 1958, he also held the positions of Premier of the Executive Yuan and Governor of the Central Bank. Hsu, with his extensive banking experience, served as the Minister of Finance from 1954 to 1958 before assuming the role of Governor of the Central Bank in 1960.

In 1958, Yu Hung-chun was faced with impeachment from the Control Yuan. Chiang Kai-shek thus nominated Vice President Chen Cheng to concurrently assume the position of Premier of the Executive Yuan on June 30. Upon assuming Premiership, Chen Cheng endeavored to establish his credibility and consolidate his power in the Executive Yuan in part because "the economy was the most important battlefield in Chen Cheng's competition with Chiang Ching-kuo to succeed Chiang Kai-shek" (Wu, 2005, p. 63). To this end, Chen Cheng sought to weaken the influence of his predecessor Yu Hung-chun and those affiliated with the presidential residence faction (Wu, 2005, p. 63). Furthermore, Chen Cheng allied himself with another group of technocrats who had weak ties to the influential factions within the KMT, such as Yin Chung-jung and Yen Chia-kan (Wu, 2005, p. 75). In early 1958, Chen Cheng convened a committee focusing on foreign exchange reforms. In the committee, Yin Chung-jung, the Secretary General of the Economic Stability Committee, supported trade and exchange rate reforms, but faced resistance from the majority, including Primer Yu Hung-chun, Minister of Finance Hsu P.Y., and Minister of Economic Affairs Kiang Piao (Irwin, 2021; Kuo and Myers, 2012). However, after Yen Chia-kan's return from the United States, he also backed the proposed reforms. In the end, Chen Cheng aligned himself with Yin Chung-jung and Yen Chia-kan, resulting in the implementation of foreign exchange reforms that marked Taiwan's shift from import substitution industrialization (ISI) to export-oriented industrialization (EOI) in economic development.

Despite being a loyalist of the Whampoa faction, Chen Cheng was not fully trusted by Chiang Kai-shek, mainly because he was perceived as a potential successor in the 1950s. Upon his assuming the role of Premier in 1958, Chen Cheng's relationship with Chiang Kai-shek quickly grew strained, particularly regarding the appointment of cabinet members, notably the Vice President of the Executive Yuan and the Minister of Education (Chen, 2013). By 1960, Chiang Kai-shek had already served two consecutive terms as President of the Republic of China and constitutionally could not serve another term. This led to widespread calls for an election and a "handover" to Chen Cheng. In 1960, the National Assembly amended the "Temporary Provisions for Mobilizing the Counterinsurgency Period" (*dongyuan kanluan shiqi linshi tiaokuan*), effectively eliminating the term limits for the President and Vice President. Despite receiving another nomination from Chiang Kai-shek for the Premier of the Executive Yuan, an already disappointed Chen Cheng made several attempts to resign, citing health issues. However, Chiang Kai-shek only granted him a leave of absence and refused his resignation.

It was not until the Ninth Congress of the KMT in 1963 that Chiang chose to revamp the Executive Yuan. This decision was likely motivated by his aim to further weaken the power of the Executive Yuan under the leadership of Chen Cheng. Notably, many candidates recommended by Chen Cheng for the Executive Yuan were excluded from Chiang's nomination list, resulting in their failure to be elected as CC members of the KMT at the Ninth Congress in 1963 (Su, 2017). Upon receiving Chiang's nomination list at 8:00 AM, Chen Cheng was deeply dismayed and chose not to attend the morning meeting (Su, 2017). In November, Chiang received Chen Cheng's resignation as Premier.

Following that, Chiang nominated Yen Chia-kan to take over the position of the Premier of the Executive Yuan from Chen Cheng. One crucial consideration for this appointment was Yen's technocratic background and limited connections to existing KMT factions, which would not impede Chiang's plan to pass on power to his son, Chiang Ching-kuo. As Wu (2005, p. 78) notes, Yen garnered Chiang Kai-shek's trust primarily due to his lack of personal political ambitions:

> He was cautious, maintained a low profile, and was good at mediating among bureaucrats. This convinced the Chiangs that Yen held no political ambitions and enabled him to win the trust of the Chiangs ... Beginning in the late 1950s, Yen was one of the few persons who could make suggestions directly to Chiang Kai-shek. This position allowed him to play a crucial role in persuading Chiang to accept the economic reforms during the late 1950s and early 1960s.

As it turned out, Yen proved to be a pivotal figure in the power transition from Chiang Kai-shek to Chiang Ching-kuo. In 1966, he ascended to the position of Vice President of the Republican of China, subsequently assuming the presidency following Chiang Kai-shek's passing in 1975. However, Yen's presidency was short-lived, spanning a mere three years. Recognizing the importance of a smooth power transition, Yen resigned from his position, throwing his support behind Chiang Ching-kuo for the role of President.

In 1969, Chiang Ching-kuo took on the role of Vice Premier of the Executive Yuan, aiming to wield his influence over economic policies. He set out to undermine the remaining influence of the presidential residence faction. As a result, Hsu P.Y. stepped down from his dual roles as the head of the Foreign Exchange Trade Review Committee and the Governor of the Central Bank of China. As Chiang Kai-shek entered his final years, Chiang Ching-kuo was appointed as the Premier of the Executive Yuan in 1972 in preparation for the upcoming succession. Despite pressure from Madame Chiang, Chiang Ching-kuo resisted appointing Kung Ling-kan, Kung Hsiang-hsi's eldest son, as the Minister of Finance (Yu, 2009, chapter 3). Furthermore, Chiang Ching-kuo sought to curb the policy influence of certain technocrats whose power was rapidly expanding. Li Kwoh-ting, a prominent figure in Taiwan's economic policies, held several leadership positions over the years in the Executive Yuan. From 1965 to 1969, he held the position of Minister of Economic Affairs, during which he cultivated a dense network of technocrats and gained considerable influence in the Executive Yuan. As Wu (2005, p. 76) points out, "when Chiang Ching-kuo began to take over economic affairs, K.T. Li had already consolidated his reputation and position as the leading economic bureaucrat. He was so influential that there was a rumor of a 'K.T. faction.' Li thus became an obstacle and threat to Ching-kuo's efforts to build up his own forces. Chiang Ching-kuo's strategy when he assumed the office of vice premier was to reshuffle the bureaucrats by replacing the veteran K.T. Li with a younger bureaucrat." In the 1969 cabinet reshuffle, Li assumed the role of Minister of Finance, despite his impressive track record at the Ministry of Economic Affairs (Yu, 2009, chapter 3). Chiang Ching-kuo appointed S. Y. Dao as the Minister of Economic Affairs, and following the unfortunate passing of S. Y. Dao a few months later, Sun Yun-suan succeeded him in that role.

To the surprise of many ruling elites, Chiang Ching-kuo advanced the "reinventing and defending Taiwan" (*gexin baotai*) policy, aiming to promote more Taiwan-born cadres into the top echelon of the KMT. Indeed, Chiang Ching-kuo's effort to promote Taiwan-born cadres could, to a degree, co-opt Taiwanese elites into the KMT and channel their participation demands (Dickson, 1996). Perhaps more importantly, this calculated strategy served to counterbalance the conservative forces within the KMT leadership, particularly the veteran cadres (Li, 2001, p. 112). In essence, this approach can be viewed as a "coalition of the weak" strategy (Shih, 2022), by creating a ruling coalition with relatively weak figures, such as those with narrow political networks or those inexperienced in national-level politics.

In Chiang Ching-kuo's new cabinet, approximately 35 percent of the cabinet members were Taiwanese (Jheng, 2006, p. 145). Notably, Hsu Ching-chung, a Taiwan-born politician, was appointed as Vice Premier. The cabinet also included other Taiwanese members, such as three ministers with less established track records, namely Lien Cheng-tung, Lee Lien-chun, and Lee Teng-hui, as well as Interior Minister Lin Jin-sheng and Transport and Communications Minister Kao Yu-shu. The 11th Party Congress of 1976 marked the triumph of Chiang Ching-kuo's "localization" (ben tu hua) policy. As shown in Figure 8, the share of Taiwanese elites in the CC expanded from 6 percent in the 1969 10th Party Congress to 16.7 percent in the 1976 11th Party Congress. More remarkably, the proportion of Taiwanese cadres in the Central Standing Committee (CSC) surged to 22.7 percent in the 11th Party Congress of 1976, a considerable increase from less than 10 percent in the 10th Party Congress of 1969 (Jheng, 2006, pp. 120–123).

Following the same logic, Sun Yun-suan was appointed as the Premier of the Executive Yuan during 1978–1984 and was designated by Chiang Ching-kuo as his successor primarily because he was a technocrat and lacked political ambition (Wu, 2005).[59] After Sun Yun-suan suffered a stroke in 1984, Chiang Ching-kuo nominated Lee Teng-hui, a Taiwanese technocrat, as the Vice

---

[59] Chiang Ching-kuo was also attentive to the actions of his loyalists and was resolute in thwarting their attempts to build up a dense informal network. Wang Sheng, Chiang Ching-kuo's confidant and the head of the General Political Warfare Department in the Ministry of National Defense, also led "the Liu Shao-Kang Office," a policy advisory body consisting of top leaders from the Party, government, and military. When Chiang Ching-kuo's health deteriorated

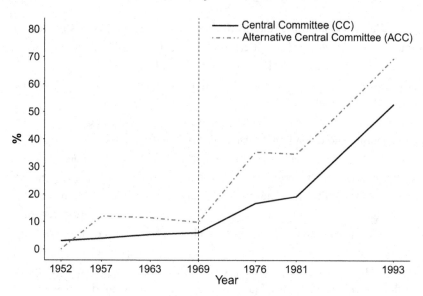

Figure 8 The share of Taiwanese in the KMT's CC and ACC.
Source: Jheng (2006)

President candidate during the plenum. Compared to other competitors, such as Lin Yang-kang and Chiu Chuang-huan, the dark horse Lee was favored by Chiang Ching-kuo largely due to his technocratic background and a perceived lack of strong factional ties with other influential party elites (Wu, 2005, p. 78).

4.4 Elite Composition and Taiwan's Economic Transition

Drawing upon the publicly available information concerning the KMT's Party congresses and Party elites (Huang and Hao, 1987; Li, 1993b, 1994; Liu, 1989, 2005), we have identified the organizational affiliations each member of the KMT Central Committee represented during every Party congress after 1952. This analytical approach enables us to ascertain whether a Central Committee member was affiliated with local governments, the military, the central government (i.e., the Executive Yuan), or the central Party apparatus of the KMT during the time of each Party congress.

---

in the early 1980s, "the Liu Shao-Kang Office" gained increasing influence in the policy-making process. They "tried to keep him [Chiang Ching-kuo] from having to make difficult decisions" and "only presented very difficult issues to him" (Marks, 2016, p. 268). As Wang Sheng endeavored to build his "political warfare (*zheng zhan*)" faction and amassed considerable power within the regime, Chiang Ching-kuo became increasingly concerned. In 1983, he disbanded "the Liu Shao-Kang Office" and ousted Wang Sheng to Paraguay to be the ambassador. At the second plenum of the 12th CC in 1984, it came as no surprise that Wang Sheng was removed from the CSC. At the same time, while the share of military leaders clearly shrank in the CSC due to Wang Sheng's demotion, more technocrats were elevated into the CSC (Yeh, 2007, pp. 107–108).

In our analysis, we focus on the relative changes in the share of the representatives from the Executive Yuan and the representatives from local and social authorities in the Central Committee. The representatives of the Executive Yuan primarily include the Premier, the Vice Premier, the Secretary-General, the ministers, and those who served in directly affiliated institutions of the Executive Yuan, such as the Taiwan Economic Stabilization Committee and the International Economic Cooperation and Development Committee. The local and social representatives mainly refer to the CC members who held positions in the Taiwan Province, "Fujian" Province, and lower-levels of local government. Notably, there were CC members who did not hold posts in Party, government, or military agencies. This group includes entrepreneurs, university professors, and overseas Chinese. We classify all these social figures as local and social representatives.

To a large extent, Taiwan's economic rise after World War II can be attributed to a pivot toward export-oriented economic polices during the 1958–1963 period (Haggard and Pang, 1994). This transition to an export-led growth strategy was by no means inevitable. The conservative forces, including the ministries within the Executive Yuan, SOEs, and the military, were beneficiaries of the import substitution industrialization (ISI) model (Haggard, 1990; Kuo and Myers, 2012). It was only with the erosion of the conservative camp's influence that Taiwan embarked on the trajectory of export-led growth (Haggard, 1990).

During this period of policy transformation, there was a notable decrease in the representation of Executive Yuan members (i.e., central technocrats) within the KMT's Central Committee, declining from 30 percent in 1952 to 19 percent in 1963. As discussed previously, this shift was in part driven by Chen Cheng's intention to undermine the influence of the presidential residence faction in the Executive Yuen and Chiang Kai-shek's aim to curtail the power base of Chen Cheng, who was perceived as his successor and emerged as a potential competitor of his son. In the meantime, the proportion of local and social representatives in the KMT's Central Committee – including local officials, as well as native Taiwanese businessmen and notables – surged from 9 percent in 1952 to 21 percent in 1963, indicating the rising influence of local, pro–private sector representation. Correspondingly, between 1963 and 1972, Taiwan's average annual growth reached a breakneck 10.9 percent, fueled largely by private sector–dominated export growth (Cheng, 2001).

As displayed in Panel A of Figure 9, the share of Executive Yuan representatives in the KMT's Central Committee (CC) witnessed an increase, reaching 23 percent in 1969 and further rising to 26.5 percent in 1976. Meanwhile, the representation of local representatives decreased to 18 percent in 1969 and remained

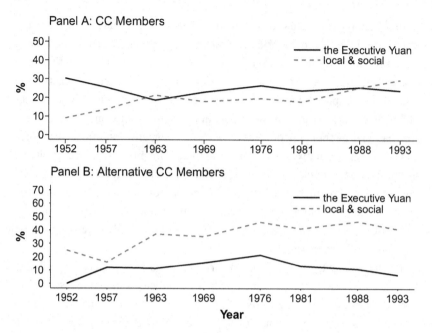

Figure 9 Composition of the KMT's CC and ACC.

at 19.7 percent in 1976. In the aftermath of the 1973 Oil Crisis, which dealt a serious blow to Taiwan's economy, the Fourth Plenary Session of the 10th KMT Party Congress, convened on November 12, 1973, announced the "Ten Major Projects." These projects required a leading role for the government. The expanding influence of the Executive Yuan facilitated more proactive government intervention in terms of advancing large-scale infrastructure projects, including both the "Ten Major Projects" and the subsequent "Twelve Major Projects" launched in 1977.

In the 1980s, Taiwan witnessed further economic liberalization, including tariff reductions, industrial upgrading, financial liberalization, SOE privatization, and the launch of the Hsinchu Science-Based Industrial Park (HSBIP) (Hsueh, Hsu, and Perkins, 2001; Pao, Wu, and Pan, 2008). During this period, the share of local and social elites in the KMT CC expanded to 26 percent at the KMT's 13th Party Congress in 1988, indicating their growing influence in the political arena. Among the alternate members of the Central Committee, the percentage of local and social representatives is much higher than the percentage of representatives from the Executive Yuan. As shown in Panel B of Figure 9, local and social representatives account for 46.67 percent, while the Executive Yuan representatives account for 11.11 percent.

It is worth noting that our measurement may potentially underestimate the political influence wielded by local and social elites, as many of them assume roles in supervisory branches, such as the National Assembly and the Legislative Yuan. To enhance our understanding of the power dynamics between the Executive Yuan and local and social representatives within the KMT Central Committee during Taiwan's authoritarian era, we propose a broader definition of "local and social representatives." This broader definition, in addition to our previously defined local and societal representatives, incorporates CC members from the "central" supervisory organizations who concurrently held positions in local and social agencies.[60]

Starting from 1969, Taiwan initiated the election of additional representatives to the National Assembly and the Legislative Yuan, attracting a broad spectrum of entrepreneurs, social workers, and university professors to the central supervisory bodies. This led to a steady increase in the representation of local and social elites in the KMT Central Committee. Taking this into account, it becomes evident that local and social elites constituted one-third of the KMT Central Committee in 1988. While acknowledging the undoubtedly multifaceted nature of Taiwan's liberalization policies, the steady representation of local and social interests within the KMT Central Committee provided reformist leaders and technocrats in the regime with natural allies in policy debates.

5 Concluding Remarks

This Element sheds light on the intriguing economic decentralization in mainland China, a politically centralized state. It highlights the critical role of the intra-elite conflicts between the authoritarian ruler and the ruling elites within the state in shaping economic policies. The authoritarian ruler, in an attempt to curb the influence of the ruling elites, pursued decentralization as a strategic response. A key turning point came with the Cultural Revolution, which, being partly instigated by these elite conflicts, substantially reoriented the composition of the elite selectorate in favor of local interests over central agencies. This realignment, which was cemented by a relatively lower turnover in the subsequent years, set the Chinese leadership on a path of decentralization during the 1980s. The resurgence of central officials in the Central Committee, however, reversed this trend, leading to a course of economic centralization from the mid-1990s to present.

---

[60] For instance, some representatives in the "central" supervisory bodies were known as "eternal national representatives" (*wannian guodai*), who were only representatives without any additional roles in society or at the local level. Therefore, they would not be considered as broadly defined local and social representatives in our analysis. However, if CC members from the central supervisory bodies also held positions at local and social agencies, they would be regarded as broadly defined local and social representatives.

The analysis in this Element highlights a political mechanism – elite reshuffling – that can steer even authoritarian regimes to a path toward decentralization. In the case of China, both exogenous shocks and endogenous processes led to a change in the composition of the CC elite, which reoriented the top leadership's incentives to either pursue decentralization to appease provincial interests, or advocate for centralization policies backed by the central bureaucracy. Therefore, the composition of the ruling party elite drove the top leadership to pursue either centralization or decentralization policies. This is analogous to how certain structures of party systems, which are endogenous to elite power dynamics, can sustain federalist institutions in democratic settings. The stickiness of elite composition across different periods lent additional weight to the stability of elite policy preferences.

Despite the turmoil of the Cultural Revolution, the wholesale removal of State Council officials and the ensuing domination by provincial officials in the Central Committee committed the post-Mao leadership to pursue decentralization policies throughout much of the 1980s. The sustained decentralization in the medium term paved the way for a series of reforms in the 1970s and the 1980s that fostered growth, including fiscal decentralization and the rapid proliferation of TVEs. Our findings indicate that the dominance of local officials in the Central Committee probably made these policies sustainable in the medium term. The flip side of the same coin was that two decades of decentralization undermined the central government's fiscal and financial capacity, preventing it from dictating investment patterns.

However, during the 1980s, senior leaders of the State Council vigorously reconstructed the central bureaucracy, and the rising complexity of economic demands rendered their arguments for a larger central bureaucracy more compelling. Following several rounds of turnovers in the 1980s and early 1990s, the presence of central bureaucrats in the Central Committee finally paralleled that of their local counterparts, effectively reversing the dramatic reorientation brought about by the Cultural Revolution. By the early 1990s, the pursuit of centrist policies was no longer such a politically challenging proposition. In the 1990s and 2000s, the capacity of the central state multiplied with fiscal and banking centralization successively, which endowed the state banks with tremendous firepower with which to finance central investment and industrial policies (Shih, 2008).

Given the status quo of central dominance both politically and economically, credible decentralization spurring local policy and reform initiatives is an unlikely path for reform in the foreseeable future. In fact, the opposite might be unfolding. Recognizing that the central government will continue to control the lion's share of economic resources in the near future, local governments may choose to forgo local initiatives aimed at fostering growth and instead focus on lobbying activities or demonstrating loyalty to the central leadership, with the aim of securing a larger slice of central resources. For instance, to achieve a certain growth or investment target, local officials may likely find it more expedient to devise a multi-billion RMB urban development plan. The approval of this plan would entitle local authorities to billions in bank loans and bond issuance, rather than attracting private and foreign investors with tax breaks and market access. In such an environment, genuine reform requires the central government to overcome vested interests and self-impose constraints on its own role in allocating economic resources. A strong leadership will need to enact credible and sustainable policies that allow private actors to control a large share of economic resources, instead of relegating private capital to a small corner of the financial system.

Our research findings extend beyond the specific context of mainland China, as evidenced by the examination of a shadow case – Taiwan under the KMT's authoritarian rule. In Taiwan, similar dynamics were at play, where the composition of the ruling party elite was also linked with policy orientation. Taiwan's economic liberalization, particularly the shift from an import substitution industrialization policy to an export-led growth strategy in the late 1950s and early 1960s, coincided with a notable decline in the political clout of the Executive Yuan representatives, the central technocrats, in the KMT's Central Committee. Our analysis demonstrates that the waning influence of the Executive Yuan was essentially a product of the dynamics of elite conflicts. The intentions of key figures like Chen Cheng to undermine the conservative forces in the Executive Yuan, and Chiang Kai-shek's aim to limit the power base of Chen Cheng were significant driving forces for this shift. Furthermore, after Chiang Ching-kuo was appointed as the Premier of the Executive Yuan in 1972, he strategically weakened the power of experienced economic technocrats and replaced them with younger technocrats with narrower political networks. This strategic maneuver made the trend of economic liberalization less likely to be reversed, despite some signs of economic centralization such as government-initiated investment projects following the 1973 Oil Crisis.

It is crucial to recognize that during the implementation of economic decentralization or liberalization policies, both mainland China and Taiwan were characterized by highly centralized states wielding significant control over society. Economic decentralization served as an engine for economic growth by channeling resources to the private sector. However, in both instances, the state managed to preserve its political authority, ensuring a measured pace of economic decentralization. From a comparative perspective, the failure of decentralization policies in many other countries may be attributable to the initial weakness of their central states. The implementation of decentralization measures further eroded the state capacity, resulting in a situation that spiraled out of control.

Our elite-centric approach can contribute to understanding the emergence and sustainability of federalism in general, or economic decentralization in particular, across broader contexts. In the case of the United States, Riker's seminal work on federalism views "federalism as a bargain between prospective national leaders and officials of constituent governments for the purpose of aggregating territory, the better to collect taxes and raise armies" (Riker, 1964, p. 11). In this vein, Filippov, Ordeshook, and Shvetsova (2004) reveal that the bargaining dynamics between national and regional elites shape the stability of federal systems in countries like Australia, Canada, Germany, and India. Likewise, in the case of Mexico, Diaz-Cayeros (2006) demonstrates that elite bargaining and compromises led to party centralization and fiscal centralization. Nevertheless, this line of research focuses primarily on how the institutional landscape (e.g., party systems) structures the incentives of political elites in the bargaining process rather than exploring how the distribution of elite power sets the bargaining process in motion and ultimately reshapes these institutions. Future research should recognize the endogenous nature of institutions and delve into elite power dynamics in the analysis.

For the literature on credible decentralization in authoritarian regimes or weakly institutionalized democracies, this Element points to avenues for future research. While institutional changes, which are often the results of political processes, remain important, it would be fruitful to also examine the impacts of political calculations and shocks on economic outcomes such as decentralization and redistribution. To be sure, this perspective is in line with the focus on political shocks or "critical junctures" that is central to much of the path dependence literature (e.g., Collier and Collier, 1991; Mahoney, 2000). Unlike in established democracies, where political coalitions formed during the early modern period or during the Great Depression led to the development of relatively stable institutions, the institutions and policy tendencies in authoritarian regimes and weak democracies were much more malleable. Thus, even in the medium term, short-term political calculus and struggles can reshape federalist or redistribution regimes (e.g., Albertus, 2015). We hope that the next wave of comparative scholarship will refine our understanding of the types of political conflicts and calculations that can lead to lasting changes in economic policies.

References

Acemoglu, Daron, and James A. Robinson. 2012. *Why Nations Fail: The Origins of Power, Prosperity and Poverty*. New York: Crown Publishing Group.

Albertus, Michael. 2015. *Autocracy and Redistribution*. Cambridge: Cambridge University Press.

Albertus, Michael, Sofia Fenner, and Dan Slater. 2018. *Coercive Distribution*. Cambridge: Cambridge University Press.

Andersen, David, and Jørgen Møller. 2019. "The Transhistorical Tension between Bureaucratic Autonomy and Political Control." *Political Studies Review* 17(3):284–295.

Ang, Yuen Yuen. 2016. *How China Escaped the Poverty Trap*. Ithaca: Cornell University Press.

Ang, Yuen Yuen. 2020. *China's Gilded Age: The Paradox of Economic Boom and Vast Corruption*. Cambridge: Cambridge University Press.

Ashton, Basil, Kenneth Hill, Alan Piazza, and Robin Zeitz. 1984. "Famine in China, 1958–61." *Population and Development Review* 10(4):613–645.

Bahry, Donna. 2005. "The New Federalism and the Paradoxes of Regional Sovereignty in Russia." *Comparative Politics* 37(2): 127–146.

Barnett, A. Doak. 1960. *Communist China and Asia*. New York: Harper and Brothers.

Bednar, Jenna. 2003. The Madisonian Scheme to Control the National Government. In *James Madison: The Theory and Practice of Republican Government*, ed. Samuel Kernell. Stanford: Stanford University Press, pp. 217–242.

Bednar, Jenna, William Eskridge, and John Ferejohn. 2001. A Political Theory of Federalism. In *Constitutions and Constitutionalism*, ed. John Ferejohn, Jack Rakove, and Jonathan Riley. Cambridge: Cambridge University Press, pp. 217–242.

Beramendi, Pablo, Mark Dincecco, and Melissa Rogers. 2019. "Intra-Elite Competition and Long-Run Fiscal Development." *The Journal of Politics* 81(1):49–65.

Bernstein, Thomas P. 2013. Resilience and Collapse in China and the Soviet Union. In *Why Communism Did Not Collapse: Understanding Authoritarian Regime Resilience in Asia and Europe*, ed. Martin Dimitrov. New York: Cambridge University Press, pp. 40–63.

Bersch, Katherine, and Francis Fukuyama. 2023. "Defining Bureaucratic Autonomy." *Annual Review of Political Science* 26: 213–232. DOI: https://doi.org/10.1146/annurev-polisci-051921-102914.

Blanchard, Olivier, and Andrei Shleifer. 2001. "Federalism with and without Political Centralization: China Versus Russia." *IMF Staff Papers* 48: 171–179.

Bo, Yibo. 1991. *Ruogan Zhongda Shijian yu Juece de Huigu (Selection from Reflections on Certain Major Decisions and Events)*. Beijing: Central Party School Publisher.

Bo, Zhiyue. 1996. "Economic Performance and Political Mobility: Chinese Provincial Leaders." *Journal of Contemporary China* 5(12):135–154.

Boix, Carles, and Milan W. Svolik. 2013. "The Foundations of Limited Authoritarian Government: Institutions, Commitment, and Power-Sharing in Dictatorships." *The Journal of Politics* 75(2):300–316.

Brahm, Laurence J. 2002. *Zhu Rongji and the Transformation of Modern China*. Singapore: Wiley.

Bremmer, Ian. 2010. *The End of the Free Market: Who Wins the War between States and Corporations?* New York: Portfolio.

Brennan, Geoffrey, and James M. Buchanan. 1980. *The Power to Tax: Analytic Foundations of a Fiscal Constitution*. Cambridge: Cambridge University Press.

Brødsgaard, Kjeld Erik. 2012. "Politics and Business Group Formation in China: The Party in Control?" *The China Quarterly* 211:624–648.

Buchanan, James M. 1995. "Federalism as an Ideal Political Order and an Objective for Constitutional Reform." *Publius: The Journal of Federalism* 25(2):19–28.

Bueno de Mesquita, Bruce, Alastair Smith, James D. Morrow, and Randolph M. Siverson. 2003. *The Logic of Political Survival*. Cambridge: Massachusetts Institute of Technology Press.

Burns, John P. 1987. "China's Nomenklatura System." *Problems of Communism* 36:36–51.

Cai, Hongbin, and Daniel Treisman. 2004. "State Corroding Federalism." *Journal of Public Economics* 88(3–4):819–843.

Cai, Hongbin, and Daniel Treisman. 2006. "Did Government Decentralization Cause China's Economic Miracle?" *World Politics* 58(4):505–535.

Chandler, Alfred D. 1962. *Strategy and Structure: Chapters in the History of the American Industrial Enterprise*. Cambridge: Massachusetts Institute of Technology Press.

Chen, Hongmin. 2013. "An Exploration of the Relationship between Chiang Kai-shek and Chen Cheng during the Taiwan Period (1949–1965)" (Taiwan shiqi Jiang Jieshi yu Chen Cheng guanxi tanwei). *Modern Chinese History Studies (jindaishi yanjiu)* (2):4–29.

Chen, Yun. 2011a. Adjusting the National Economy and Adhering to Proportional Development (Tiaozheng Guomin Jingji, Jianchi an Bili Fazhan). In *Sanzhong quanhui yilai zhongyao wenxian xuanbian shang ce (Collection of Important Documents since the Third Plenum. Volume 1)*, ed. CCP Central Document Research Office. Beijing: People's Publishing House.

Chen, Yun. 2011b. Economic Situations and Lessons (Jingji Xingshi yu Jingyan Jiaoxun). In *Sanzhong quanhui yilai zhongyao wenxian xuanbian shang ce (Collection of Important Documents since the Third Plenum. Volume 1)*, ed. CCP Central Document Research Office. Beijing: People's Publishing House.

Cheng, Tun-Jen. 2001. "Transforming Taiwan's Economic Structure in the 20th Century." *The China Quarterly* 165:19–36.

Chibber, Pradeep, and Ken Kollman. 2004. *The Formation of National Party Systems: Federalism and Party Competition in Canada, Great Britain, India, and the United States*. Princeton: Princeton University Press.

Choi, Eun Kyong. 2012. "Patronage and Performance: Factors in the Political Mobility of Provincial Leaders in Post-Deng China." *The China Quarterly* 212:965–981.

Chu, Wan-Wen. 2017. *Taiwan Zhanhou Jingji Fazhan de Yuanqi: Houjin Fazhan de Weihe yu Ruhe (The Origin of Post-war Economic Development in Taiwan: Why and How did the Late Development Occur?)*. Taipei: Linking Publishing Company. https://searchworks.stanford.edu/view/11925318.

Chung, Jae Ho. 1994. "Beijing Confronting the Provinces: The 1994 Tax-Sharing Reform and Its Implications for Central–Provincial Relations in China." *China Information* 9(2–3):1–23.

Coale, Ansley. 1981. "Population Trends, Population Policy, and Population Studies in China." *Population and Development Review* 8(2):85–97.

Collier, David. 2011. "Understanding Process Tracing." *PS: Political Science & Politics* 44(4):823–830.

Collier, Ruth Berins, and David Collier. 1991. *Shaping the Political Arena: Critical Junctures, the Labor Movement, and Regime Dynamics in Latin America*. Princeton: Princeton University Press.

"Contemporary China's Economic Management" Compilation Group, ed. 1996. *Zhonghua renmin gongheguo jingji guanli dashiji (Chronicle of the Economic Management of the People's Republic of China)*. Beijing: China Economics Publishers.

Cui, Wunian. 2003. *Wo de 83 ge Yue (My 83 Months)*. Hong Kong: Ko Man Publishing Co.

Davoodi, Hamid, and Heng-fu Zou. 1998. "Fiscal Decentralization and Economic Growth: A Cross-Country Study." *Journal of Urban Economics* 43(2):244–257.

Deng, Liqun. 2005. *Shi'erge Chunqiu: 1975–1987 (Twelve Springs and Autumns: 1975–1987)*. Hong Kong: Bozhi Publisher.

Deng, Xiaoping. 1993. *Selected Works of Deng Xiaoping: Volume 3 (Deng Xiaoping Wenxuan di san juan)*. Beijing: People's Publishing House.

Deng, Xiaoping. 1994. *Selected Works of Deng Xiaoping: Volume 2 (Deng Xiaoping Wenxuan di er juan)*. Beijing: People's Publishing House.

Diaz-Cayeros, Alberto. 2006. *Federalism, Fiscal Authority, and Centralization in Latin America*. Cambridge: Cambridge University Press.

Dickson, Bruce J. 1993. "The Lessons of Defeat: The Reorganization of the Kuomintang on Taiwan, 1950–52." *The China Quarterly* 133:56–84.

Dickson, Bruce J. 1996. The Kuomintang before Democratization: Organizational Change and the Role of Elections. In *Taiwan's Electoral Politics and Democratic Transition: Riding the Third Wave*, ed. Hung-Mao Tien. New York: M. E. Sharpe, pp. 42–78.

Dikötter, Frank. 2010. *Mao's Great Famine: The History of China's Most Devastating Catastrophe, 1958–62*. A&C Black.

Dikötter, Frank. 2013. *The Tragedy of Liberation: A History of the Chinese Revolution, 1945–1957*. New York: Bloomsbury.

Dikötter, Frank. 2016. "The Silent Revolution: Decollectivization from Below During the Cultural Revolution." *The China Quarterly* 227:796–811.

Dong, Guoqiang, and Andrew G. Walder. 2012. "From Truce to Dictatorship: Creating a Revolutionary Committee in Jiangsu." *The China Journal* 68(1):1–31.

Donnithorne, Audrey. 1972. "China's Cellular Economy: Some Economic Trends since the Cultural Revolution." *The China Quarterly* 52:605–619.

Donnithorne, Audrey. 1980. "Aspects of Neo-Liuist Economic Policy." *The Australian Journal of Chinese Affairs* (3):27–39.

Donnithorne, Audrey, and Nicholas R. Lardy. 1976. "Centralization and Decentralization in China's Fiscal Management." *The China Quarterly* (66):328–354.

Eastman, Lloyd E. 1984. *Seeds of Destruction. Nationalist China in War and Revolution 1937–1949*. Stanford: Stanford University Press.

Eaton, Sarah. 2016. *The Advance of the State in Contemporary China: State-Market Relations in the Reform Era*. Cambridge: Cambridge University Press.

Edin, Maria. 2003. "State Capacity and Local Agent Control in China: CCP Cadre Management from a Township Perspective." *The China Quarterly* 173:35–52.

Enikolopov, Ruben, and Ekaterina Zhuravskaya. 2007. "Decentralization and Political Institutions." *Journal of Public Economics* 91(11–12):2261–2290.

Fan, Gang, Wen Hai, and Wing Thye Woo. 1996. Decentralized Socialism and Macroeconomic Stability: Lessons from China in the 1980s. In *Inflation and Growth in China: Proceedings of a Conference Held in Beijing, China, May 10–12, 1995*, ed. Manuel Guitián and Robert Mundell. Washington, DC: International Monetary Fund.

Feng, Xianzhi, and Chongji Jin, eds. 2013. *Mao Zedong Zhuan (Mao Zedong's Biography*. Beijing: Zhongyang Wenxian Chubanshe.

Feng, Xianzhi, and Hui Feng, eds. 2013a. *Mao Zedong Nianpu di liu juan (A Chronicle of Mao Zedong: Volume 6*. Beijing: Zhongyang Wenxian Chubanshe.

Feng, Xianzhi, and Hui Feng, eds. 2013b. *Mao Zedong Nianpu di wu juan (A Chronicle of Mao Zedong: Volume 5*. Beijing: Zhongyang Wenxian Chubanshe.

Fewsmith, Joseph. 2001. *China since Tiananmen: The Politics of Transition*. Cambridge: Cambridge University Press.

Fewsmith, Joseph. 2016. *Dilemmas of Reform in China: Political Conflict and Economic Debate*. Armonk, NY: M. E. Sharpe.

Field, Robert Michael. 1986. "The Performance of Industry during the Cultural Revolution: Second Thoughts." *The China Quarterly* 108:625–642.

Filippov, Mikhail, Peter C. Ordeshook, and Olga Shvetsova. 2004. *Designing Federalism: A Theory of Self-Sustainable Federal Institutions*. Cambridge: Cambridge University Press.

Finan, Frederico, Benjamin A. Olken, and Rohini Pande. 2017. The Personnel Economics of the Developing State. In *Handbook of Economic Field Experiments (Volume 2)*, ed. Abhijit Vinayak Banerjee and Esther Duflo. Amsterdam: Elsevier, pp. 467–514.

Fukuyama, Francis. 2011. *The Origins of Political Order: From Prehuman Times to the French Revolution*. New York: Farrar, Straus and Giroux.

Gallagher, Mary E., and Jonathan K. Hanson. 2015. "Power Tool or Dull Blade? Selectorate Theory for Autocracies." *Annual Review of Political Science* 18:367–385.

Gandhi, Jennifer. 2008. *Political Institutions under Dictatorship*. New York: Cambridge University Press.

Gao, Hua. 2018. *How the Red Sun Rose: The Origin and Development of the Yan'an Rectification Movement, 1930–1945*. Hong Kong: The Chinese University of Hong Kong Press.

Garfias, Francisco. 2018. "Elite Competition and State Capacity Development: Theory and Evidence from Post-Revolutionary Mexico." *American Political Science Review* 112(2):339–357.

Garfias, Francisco. 2019. "Elite Coalitions, Limited Government, and Fiscal Capacity Development: Evidence from Bourbon Mexico." *The Journal of Politics* 81(1):94–111.

Garfias, Francisco, and Emily A. Sellars. 2021. "When State Building Backfires: Elite Coordination and Popular Grievance in Rebellion." *American Journal of Political Science* (Online First).

Garman, Christopher, Stephan Haggard, and Eliza Willis. 2001. "Fiscal Decentralization: A Political Theory with Latin American Cases." *World Politics* 53(2):205–236.

Gehlbach, Scott, and Philip Keefer. 2011. "Investment without Democracy: Ruling-Party Institutionalization and Credible Commitment in Autocracies." *Journal of Comparative Economics* 39(2):123–139.

Gehlbach, Scott, and Philip Keefer. 2012. "Private Investment and the Institutionalization of Collective Action in Autocracies: Ruling Parties and Legislatures." *The Journal of Politics* 74(2):621–635.

Gu, Longsheng. 1993. *Mao Zedong Jingji Nianpu (An Economic Chronology of Mao Zedong)*. Beijing: Central Party School Publisher.

Gurr, Ted Robert. 1988. "War, Revolution, and the Growth of the Coercive State." *Comparative Political Studies* 21(1):45–65.

Haggard, Stephan. 1990. *Pathways from the Periphery: The Politics of Growth in the Newly Industrializing Countries*. Ithaca: Cornell University Press.

Haggard, Stephan, and Chien-Kuo Pang. 1994. The Transition to Export-Led Growth in Taiwan. In *The Role of the State in Taiwan's Development*, ed. Joel D. Aberbach, David Dollar, and Kenneth L. Sokoloff. New York: M. E. Sharpe, pp. 47–89.

Harbers, Imke. 2010. "Decentralization and the Development of Nationalized Party Systems in New Democracies: Evidence from Latin America." *Comparative Political Studies* 43(5):606–627.

Heilmann, Sebastian. 2018. *Red Swan: How Unorthodox Policy-Making Facilitated China's Rise*. Hong Kong: Chinese University Press.

Hinton, William. 1966. *Fanshen: A Documentary of Revolution in a Chinese Village*. New York: Monthly Review Press.

Hsueh, Li-min, Chen-kuo Hsu, and Dwight H. Perkins. 2001. *Industrialization and the State: The Changing Role of the Taiwan Government in the*

Economy, 1945–1998. Cambridge, MA: Harvard Institute for International Development.

Huang, Meizhen, and Shengchao Hao. 1987. *Zhonghua Minguoshi: Shijian Renwu lu (History of the Republic of China: Events and Personal Records)*. Shanghai: Shanghai Renmin Chubanshe.

Huang, Yasheng. 1999. *Inflation and Investment Controls in China: The Political Economy of Central-Local Relations during the Reform Era*. Cambridge: Cambridge University Press.

Huang, Yasheng. 2008. *Capitalism with Chinese Characteristics: Entrepreneurship and the State*. Cambridge: Cambridge University Press.

Huang, Yasheng. 2012. "How Did China Take Off?" *Journal of Economic Perspectives* 26(4):147–170.

Huang, Yasheng. 2023. *The Rise and Fall of the EAST: How Exams, Autocracy, Stability, and Technology Brought China Success, and Why They Might Lead to Its Decline*. New Haven: Yale University Press.

Irwin, Douglas A. 2021. "How Economic Ideas Led to Taiwan's Shift to Export Promotion in the 1950s." Working paper. National Bureau of Economic Research.

Iyer, Lakshmi, and Anandi Mani. 2012. "Traveling Agents: Political Change and Bureaucratic Turnover in India." *Review of Economics and Statistics* 94(3):723–739.

Jaros, Kyle A. 2019. *China's Urban Champions: The Politics of Spatial Development*. Princeton: Princeton University Press.

Jheng, Wun-Syun. 2006. Jiang Jingguo yu Dangzheng Gaoceng Renshi Bentuhua (Chiang Ching-kuo's Personnel Policy on the Localization of the KMT Party and R.O.C. Government (1970–1988)). Master's thesis. National Central University Taipei.

Jia, Ruixue, Masayuki Kudamatsu, and David Seim. 2015. "Political Selection in China: The Complementary Roles of Connections and Performance." *Journal of the European Economic Association* 13(4):631–668.

Jiang, Junyan, Tianyang Xi, and Haojun Xie. 2024. "In the Shadows of Great Men: Retired Leaders and Informal Power Constraints in Autocracies." *British Journal of Political Science*.

Jiang, Tingyu. 2006. *The Long March in Multiple Perspectives (Duoshijiao Xia De Changzheng)*. Beijing: National Defence University Press.

Jin, Chongji, ed. 2015. *Zhou Enlai zhuan (Biography of Zhou Enlai)*. Beijing: Zhongyang Wenxian Chubanshe.

Jin, Hehui, Yingyi Qian, and Barry R. Weingast. 2005. "Regional Decentralization and Fiscal Incentives: Federalism, Chinese Style." *Journal of Public Economics* 89(9–10):1719–1742.

Jones, Benjamin F., and Benjamin A. Olken. 2005. "Do Leaders Matter? National Leadership and Growth since World War II." *The Quarterly Journal of Economics* 120(3):835–864.

Jones, Mark P., Pablo Sanguinetti, and Mariano Tommasi. 2000. "Politics, Institutions, and Fiscal Performance in a Federal System: An Analysis of the Argentine Provinces." *Journal of Development Economics* 61(2):305–333.

Kay, Cristóbal. 2002. "Why East Asia Overtook Latin America: Agrarian Reform, Industrialisation and Development." *Third World Quarterly* 23(6):1073–1102.

Kim, Heung-Kyu. 2004. "The Politics of Fiscal Standardization in China: Fiscal Contract Versus Tax Assignment." *Asian Perspective* 28(2):171–203.

Knight, Jack. 1992. *Institutions and Social Conflict*. Cambridge: Cambridge University Press.

Kuhn, Philip A. 1990. *Soulstealers: The Chinese Sorcery Scare of 1768*. Cambridge, MA: Harvard University Press.

Kuo, Tai-Chun, and Ramon H. Myers. 2012. *Taiwan's Economic Transformation: Leadership, Property Rights and Institutional Change 1949–1965*. Routledge.

Landry, Pierre. 2008. *Decentralized Authoritarianism in China: The Communist Party's Control of Local Elites in the Post-Mao Era*. Cambridge: Cambridge University Press.

Landry, Pierre F., Xiaobo Lü, and Haiyan Duan. 2018. "Does Performance Matter? Evaluating Political Selection along the Chinese Administrative Ladder." *Comparative Political Studies* 51(8):1074–1105.

Lardy, Nicholas R. 1975. "Centralization and Decentralization in China's Fiscal Management." *The China Quarterly* 61:25–60.

Lardy, Nicholas R. 2019. *The State Strikes Back: The End of Economic Reform in China?* Washington, DC: Peterson Institute for International Economics.

Leutert, Wendy, and Sarah Eaton. 2021. "Deepening Not Departure: Xi Jinping's Governance of China's State-Owned Economy." *The China Quarterly* 248(S1):200–221.

Levitsky, Steven, and Lucan Way. 2022. *Revolution and Dictatorship: The Violent Origins of Durable Authoritarianism*. Princeton: Princeton University Press.

Li, Haiwen. 2019. "A Clash at the Beijing Xijiao Hotel in 1976 (1976 Nian Jingxi Binguan de Yichang Jiaofeng)." *Century (Shiji)* (2):11–16.

Li, Hongbin, and Li-An Zhou. 2005. "Political Turnover and Economic Performance: The Incentive Role of Personnel Control in China." *Journal of Public Economics* 89(9–10):1743–1762.

Li, K. T. 1993a. *The Evolution of Policy Behind Taiwan's Development Success (Taiwan Jingji Fazhan Beihou de Zhengce Yanbian)*. Nanjing: Southeast University Press.

Li, Rui. 1996. *Da Yue Jin Qin Li Ji: shang juan (My Personal Experience of the Great Leap Forward: Volume 1)*. Shanghai: Shanghai yuan dong chubanshe.

Li, Songlin. 1993b. *Zhongguo Guomindang Dangshi Dacidian (Dictionary of the Kuomintang's Party History)*. Hefei: Anhui People's Publishing House.

Li, Songlin. 2001. *Wannian Jiang Jingguo (Chiang Ching-kuo in His Later Years)*. Hefei: Anhui People's Publishing House.

Li, Xing, Chong Liu, Xi Weng, and Li-An Zhou. 2019. "Target Setting in Tournaments: Theory and Evidence from China." *The Economic Journal* 129(10):2888–2915.

Li, Yun-Han. 1994. *Zhongguo guomindang zhiminglu (Directory of Office Holders of the Kuomintang)*. Taipei: Zhongguo Guomindang Zhongyang Weiyuanhui Dangshi Weiyuanhui (The Chinese Kuomintang Central Committee Party History Committee).

Lin, Justin Yifu. 2011. *Demystifying the Chinese Economy*. Cambridge: Cambridge University Press.

Lin, Justin Yifu, and Zhiqiang Liu. 2000. "Fiscal Decentralization and Economic Growth in China." *Economic Development and Cultural Change* 49(1):1–21.

Lin, Li-Wen, and Curtis J. Milhaupt. 2013. "We Are the (National) Champions: Understanding the Mechanisms of State Capitalism in China." *Stanford Law Review* 65(4):697–759.

Lin, Yunhui. 2017. *Chong kao Gao Gang, Rao Shushi "Fan Dang" Shi Jian (A Re-investigation of the "Anti-Party" Incident of Gao Gang and Rao Shushi)*. The Chinese University of Hong Kong Press.

Liu, Guoming. 1989. *Zhonghua Minguo Guomin Zhengfu Junzheng Zhiguan Renwu Zhi (Biographical Dictionary of the Military and Political Figures of the Republic of China)*. Beijing: Chunqiu Chubanshe.

Liu, Guoming. 2005. *Zhongguo Guomindang Bainian Renwu Quanshu (Biographical Dictionary of Figures in the Kuomintang's Centennial History)*. Beijing: Tuanjie Chubanshe.

Liu, Kegu, and Kang Jia. 2008. *Zhongguo Caishui Gaige Sanshinian: Qinli yu Huigu (China's Fiscal and Tax Reforms in Three Decades)*. Beijing: Economic Science Press.

Liu, Mingxing, Victor Shih, and Dong Zhang. 2022. "Revolution, State Building, and the Great Famine in China." *Political Research Quarterly*. DOI: https://doi.org/10.1177/10659129221120384.

Liu, Shaoqi. 1985. *Liu Shaoqi Xuanji xia juan (Selected Works of Liu Shaoqi: Volume 2)*. Beijing: Renmin Publishing House.

Ma, Jiesan, ed. 1991. *Dangdai Zhongguo de Xiangzhen Qiye (Contemporary China's Township and Village Enterprises)*. Beijing: Contemporary China Press.

MacFarquhar, Roderick. 1974. *The Origins of the Cultural Revolution Volume 1: Contradictions among the People, 1956–1957*. London: Oxford University Press.

MacFarquhar, Roderick. 1983. *The Origins of the Cultural Revolution Volume 2: The Great Leap Forward 1958–60*. New York: Columbia University Press.

MacFarquhar, Roderick. 1997. *The Origins of the Cultural Revolution, Volume 3: The Coming of the Cataclysm, 1961–1966*. Oxford and New York: Oxford University Press and Columbia University Press.

MacFarquhar, Roderick, and Michael Schoenhals. 2006. *Mao's Last Revolution*. Cambridge, MA: Harvard University Press.

Magaloni, Beatriz. 2008. "Credible Power-Sharing and the Longevity of Authoritarian Rule." *Comparative Political Studies* 41(4–5):715–741.

Mahoney, James. 2000. "Path Dependence in Historical Sociology." *Theory and Society* 29(4):507–548.

Mahoney, James. 2012. "The Logic of Process Tracing Tests in the Social Sciences." *Sociological Methods & Research* 41(4):570–597.

Mahoney, James, and Kathleen Thelen, eds. 2009. *Explaining Institutional Change: Ambiguity, Agency, and Power*. Cambridge: Cambridge University Press.

Manion, Melanie. 1993. *Retirement of Revolutionaries in China: Public Policies, Social Norms, Private Interests*. Princeton: Princeton University Press.

Mao, Zedong. 1977. *Mao Zedong Xuanji (Selected Works of Mao Zedong: Volume 5)*. Beijing: Renmin Publishing House.

Mao, Zedong. 1997. *Mao Zedong wenji di qi juan (Collected Writings of Mao Zedong: Volume 7)*. Beijing: Renmin Publishing House.

Mao, Zedong. 1998. *Jianguo yilai Mao Zedong wengao di shier juan (Mao Zedong's Manuscripts since the Founding of the People's Republic of China: Volume 12)*. Beijing: Zhongyang wenxian chubanshe.

Mares, Isabela, and Didac Queralt. 2015. "The Non-Democratic Origins of Income Taxation." *Comparative Political Studies* 48(14):1974–2009.

Marks, Thomas A. 2016. *Counterrevolution in China: Wang Sheng and the Kuomintang*. London: Routledge.

Maskin, Eric, Yingyi Qian, and Chenggang Xu. 2000. "Incentives, Information, and Organizational Form." *The Review of Economic Studies* 67(2): 359–378.

McCubbins, Mathew D., Roger G. Noll, and Barry R. Weingast. 1987. "Administrative Procedures as Instruments of Political Control." *The Journal of Law, Economics, and Organization* 3(2):243–277.

Meisner, Maurice. 1999. *Mao's China and After: A History of the People's Republic*. New York: The Free Press.

Meng, Anne, Jack Paine, and Robert Powell. 2023. "Authoritarian Power Sharing: Concepts, Mechanisms, and Strategies." *Annual Review of Political Science* 26:153–173.

Montinola, Gabriella, Yingyi Qian, and Barry R. Weingast. 1995. "Federalism, Chinese Style: The Political Basis for Economic Success in China." *World Politics* 48(1):50–81.

Nathan, Andrew, and Bruce Gilley. 2002. *China's New Rulers: The Secret Files*. New York: The New York Review of Books.

Nathan, Andrew J. 1973. "A Factionalism Model for CCP Politics." *The China Quarterly* 53:34–66.

Naughton, Barry. 1988. "The Third Front: Defence Industrialization in the Chinese Interior." *The China Quarterly* 115:351–386.

Naughton, Barry. 1996. *Growing Out of the Plan: Chinese Economic Reform, 1978–1993*. Cambridge: Cambridge University Press.

Naughton, Barry. 2015. The Transformation of the State Sector: SASAC, the Market Economy, and the New National Champions. In *State Capitalism, Institutional Adaptation, and the Chinese Miracle*, ed. Barry Naughton and Kellee S. Tsai. Cambridge: Cambridge University Press, pp. 46–74.

Naughton, Barry, and Kellee S. Tsai, eds. 2015. *State Capitalism, Institutional Adaptation, and the Chinese Miracle*. Cambridge: Cambridge University Press.

North, Douglass C. 1981. *Structure and Change in Economic History*. New York: W. W. Norton & Company.

North, Douglass C. 1990. *Institutions, Institutional Changes and Economic Performance*. Cambridge: Cambridge University Press.

Oates, Wallace. 1972. *Fiscal Federalism*. New York: Harcount Brace Jovanovich.

Oates, Wallace. 1999. "An Essay on Fiscal Federalism." *Journal of Economic Literature* 37(3):1120–1149.

OECD. 2009. "State Owned Enterprises in China: Reviewing the Evidence." *OECD Working Group on Privatization and Corporate Governance*.

Oi, Jean C. 1992. "Fiscal Reform and the Economic Foundations of Local State Corporatism in China." *World Politics* 45(1):99–126.

Oksenberg, Michel, and James Tong. 1991. "The Evolution of Central-Provincial Fiscal Relations in China, 1971–1984: The Formal System." *The China Quarterly* 125:1–32.

Pan, Wei. 2003. *Nongmin yu shichang (Peasants and the Market)*. Beijing: The Commercial Press.

Pao, Huei-Wen, Hsueh-Liang Wu, and Wei-Hwa Pan. 2008. "The Road to Liberalization: Policy Design and Implementation of Taiwan's Privatization." *International Economics and Economic Policy* 5:323–344.

Pearson, Margaret M., Meg Rithmire, and Kellee S. Tsai. 2022. "China's Party-State Capitalism and International Backlash: From Interdependence to Insecurity." *International Security* 47(2):135–176.

Pearson, Margaret M., Meg Rithmire, and Kellee Tsai. 2023. *The State and Capitalism in China*. Elements in Politics and Society in East Asia. Cambridge: Cambridge University Press.

Pepinsky, Thomas. 2014. "The Institutional Turn in Comparative Authoritarianism." *British Journal of Political Science* 44(3):631–653.

Pepinsky, Thomas B. 2009. *Economic Crises and the Breakdown of Authoritarian Regimes: Indonesia and Malaysia in Comparative Perspective*. Cambridge: Cambridge University Press.

Pepper, Suzanne. 1999. *Civil War in China: The Political Struggle 1945–1949*. New York: Rowman & Littlefield Publishers.

Pierson, Paul. 2004. *Politics in Time: History, Institutions, and Social Analysis*. Princeton: Princeton University Press.

Poncet, Sandra. 2005. "A Fragmented China: Measure and Determinants of Chinese Domestic Market Disintegration." *Review of International Economics* 13(3):409–430.

Qian, Yingyi. 2000. The Institutional Foundations of China's Market Transition. In *Annual World Bank Conference on Development Economics*, ed. Boris Pleskovic and Joseph E. Stiglitz. Washington, DC: The World Bank, pp. 217–242.

Qian, Yingyi, and Barry R. Weingast. 1997. "Federalism as a Commitment to Reserving Market Incentives." *Journal of Economic Perspectives* 11(4): 83–92.

Qian, Yingyi, and Chenggang Xu. 1993. "Why China's Economic Reforms Differ: The M-Form Hierarchy and Entry/Expansion of the Non-state Sector." *Economics of Transition* 1(2):135–170.

Qian, Yingyi, and Gerard Roland. 1998. "Federalism and the Soft Budget Constraint." *American Economic Review* 88(5):1143–1162.

Qian, Yingyi, Gerard Roland, and Chenggang Xu. 2006. "Coordination and Experimentation in M-Form and U-Form Organizations." *Journal of Political Economy* 114(2):366–402.

Riker, William H. 1964. *Federalism: Origin, Operation, Significance*. Boston: Little, Brown and Company.

Riker, William H. 1975. Federalism. In *Handbook of Political Science: Governmental Institutions and Processes*, ed. Fred I. Greenstein and Nelson W. Polsby. Reading: Addison-Wesley, pp. 93–172.

Riker, William H., and Ronald Schaps. 1957. "Disharmony in Federal Government." *Behavioral Science* 2(4):276–290.

Rodden, Jonathan. 2006. *Hamilton's Paradox: The Promise and Peril of Fiscal Federalism*. Cambridge: Cambridge University Press.

Rodden, Jonathan, and Erik Wibbels. 2002. "Beyond the Fiction of Federalism: Macroeconomic Management in Multitiered Systems." *World Politics* 54(4):494–531.

Rodrik, Dani. 2006. "Goodbye Washington Consensus, Hello Washington Confusion? A Review of the World Bank's Economic Growth in the 1990s: Learning from a Decade of Reform." *Journal of Economic Literature* 44(4):973–987.

Salisbury, Harrison. 1985. *The Long March: The Untold Story*. London: Macmillan.

Seybolt, Peter J. 1986. "Terror and Conformity: Counterespionage Campaigns, Rectification, and Mass Movements, 1942–1943." *Modern China* 12(1): 39–73.

Shen, Zhihua. 2008. "Zhou Enlai yu 1956 nian de fan maojin (Zhou Enlai and the Counter-Aggressive-Advance in 1956." *Shi Lin (Historical Review)* (1):88–106.

Shepsle, Kenneth A. 2006. Old Questions and New Answers about Institutions: The Riker Objection Revisited. In *The Oxford Handbook of Political Economy*, ed. Barry R. Weingast and Donald A. Wittman. New York: Oxford University Press, pp. 1031–1049.

Shi, Jianguo. 2008. "Wenge Shiqi Fangquan Gaige dui Dongbei Jingji de Yingxiang (Impact of the Reform of Power Devolution on the Industry of Northeast China during the Cultural Revolution)." *Dangdai zhongguo shi yanjiu (Contemporary China History Studies)* 15(3):74–82.

Shih, Victor. 2008. *Factions and Finance in China: Elite Conflict and Inflation*. Cambridge: Cambridge University Press.

Shih, Victor C. 2022. *Coalitions of the Weak: Elite Politics in China from Mao's Stratagem to the Rise of Xi*. Cambridge: Cambridge University Press.

Shih, Victor, Christopher Adolph, and Mingxing Liu. 2012. "Getting Ahead in the Communist Party: Explaining the Advancement of Central Committee Members in China." *American Political Science Review* 106(1):166–187.

Shih, Victor, Wei Shan, and Mingxing Liu. 2010a. The Central Committee Past and Present: A Method of Quantifying Elite Biographies. In *Contemporary Chinese Politics New Sources, Methods, and Field Strategies*, ed. Mary

Gallagher, Melanie Manion, and Alan Carlson. Cambridge: Cambridge University Press.

Shih, Victor, Wei Shan, and Mingxing Liu. 2010b. "Gauging the Elite Political Equilibrium in the CCP: A Quantitative Approach Using Biographical Data." *The China Quarterly* 201:79–103.

Shirk, Susan. 1993. *The Political Logic of Economic Reform in China*. Berkeley: University of California Press.

Shleifer, Andrei. 1997. "Government in Transition." *European Economic Review* 41(3–5):385–410.

Skocpol, Theda. 1979. *States and Social Revolutions: A Comparative Analysis of France, Russia and China*. Cambridge: Cambridge University Press.

Skocpol, Theda. 1988. "Social Revolutions and Mass Military Mobilization." *World Politics* 40(2):147–168.

Strauss, Julia. 2006. "Morality, Coercion and State Building by Campaign in the Early PRC: Regime Consolidation and After, 1949–1956." *The China Quarterly* 188:891–912.

Strauss, Julia C. 2019. *State Formation in China and Taiwan: Bureaucracy, Campaign, and Performance*. Cambridge: Cambridge University Press.

Su, Fubing, Ran Tao, and Dali Yang. 2018. Rethinking the Institutional Foundations of China's Hypergrowth. In *The Oxford Handbook of the Politics of Development*, ed. Carol Lancaster and Nicholas van de Walle. Oxford: Oxford University Press, pp. 626–651.

Su, Fubing, Ran Tao, Lu Xi, and Ming Li. 2012. "Local Officials' Incentives and China's Economic Growth: Tournament Thesis Reexamined and Alternative Explanatory Framework." *China & World Economy* 20(4): 1–18.

Su, Sheng-hsiung. 2017. The Relationship between Chen Cheng and Chiang Kai-shek: Focusing on the Resignation of the President of the Executive Yuan (1962–1965) (Chen Cheng yu Jiang Zhongzheng zhi guanxi: yi ceren xingzheng yuanzhang wei zhongxin: 1962–1965). In *Taiwan in the 1960s (1960 niandai de Taiwan)*, ed. Ko-wu Huang. Taipei: National Chiang Kai-shek Memorial Hall, pp. 173–212.

Svolik, Milan. 2012. *The Politics of Authoritarian Rule*. New York: Cambridge University Press.

Swaine, Michael Dalzell. 1986. Heavy Industry Policy under Hua Guofeng: Bureaucracy and the Policy Process. PhD Dissertation. Harvard University.

Teiwes, Frederick C. 1984. *Leadership, Legitimacy and Conflict in China: From a Charismatic Mao to the Politics of Succession*. Armonk: M. E. Sharpe.

Teiwes, Frederick C., and Warren Sun. 1999. *China's Road to Disaster: Mao, Central Politicians and Provincial Leaders in the Great Leap Forward, 1955– 59.* New York: M. E. Sharpe.

The Editorial Group of the Biography of Li Xiannian, ed. 2009. *The Biography of Li Xiannian (Li Xiannian Zhuan) (1949–1992).* Beijing: Zhongyang Wenxian Chubanshe.

Thornton, John. 2007. "Fiscal Decentralization and Economic Growth Reconsidered." *Journal of Urban Economics* 61(1):64–70.

Tiebout, Charles M. 1956. "A Pure Theory of Local Expenditures." *Journal of Political Economy* 64(5):416–424.

Tien, Hung-mao. 1989. *The Great Transition: Political and Social Change in the Republic of China.* Stanford: Hoover Institution Press.

Tirole, Jean. 1999. "Incomplete Contracts: Where Do We Stand?" *Econometrica* 67(4):741–781.

Toral, Guillermo. 2023. "How Patronage Delivers: Political Appointments, Bureaucratic Accountability, and Service Delivery in Brazil." *American Journal of Political Science* .

Treisman, Daniel. 1999. "Political Decentralization and Economic Reform: A Game-Theoretic Analysis." *American Journal of Political Science*, pp. 488–517.

Treisman, Daniel. 2015. "Income, Democracy, and Leader Turnover." *American Journal of Political Science* 59(4):927–942.

Tullock, Gordon. 1987. *Autocracy.* Dordrecht: Springer Science & Business Media.

Walder, Andrew G. 1986. *Communist Neo-traditionalism: Work and Authority in Chinese Industry.* Berkeley: University of California Press.

Walder, Andrew G. 1995. "Local Governments as Industrial Firms: An Organizational Analysis of China's Transitional Economy." *American Journal of Sociology* 101(2):263–301.

Walder, Andrew G. 2015. *China under Mao: A Revolution Derailed.* Cambridge, MA: Harvard University Press.

Walder, Andrew G. 2016. "Bending the Arc of Chinese History: The Cultural Revolution's Paradoxical Legacy." *The China Quarterly* 227:613–631.

Walker, Richard L. 1955. *China under Communism: The First Five Years.* New Haven: Yale University Press.

Walter, Carl, and Fraser Howie. 2011. *Red Capitalism: The Fragile Financial Foundation of China's Extraordinary Rise.* Singapore: John Wiley & Sons.

Wang, Chen-main Peter. 2007. A Bastion Created, a Regime Reformed, an Economy Reengineered, 1949–1970. In *Taiwan: A New History*, ed. Murray A. Rubinstein. Armonk: M. E. Sharpe, pp. 320–338.

Wang, Kejing. 1987. *Taiwan Minjian Chanye 40 nian (Taiwan's Private Indus-tries in the Past 40 Years)*. Taipei: Zili Wanbao.

Wang, Li. 2001. *Wangli Fansi Lu (Introspection of Wang Li)*. Hong Kong: Beixing Chubanshe.

Wang, Qisheng. 2003. *Dangyuan, Dangquan yu Dangzheng: 1924–1949 nian Zhongguo Guo mindang de Zuzhi Xing tai (Party Members, Party Power and Party Conflicts: The Organizational Configuration of the KMT from 1924 to 1949)*. Shanghai: Shanghai Bookstore Press.

Wedeman, Andrew H. 2003. *From Mao to Market: Rent Seeking, Local Pro-tectionism, and Marketization in China*. Cambridge: Cambridge University Press.

Wedeman, Andrew H. 2012. *Double Paradox: Rapid Growth and Rising Corruption in China*. Ithaca: Cornell University Press.

Weingast, Barry R. 1995. "The Economic Role of Political Institutions: Market-Preserving Federalism and Economic Development." *The Journal of Law, Economics, and Organization* 11(1):1–31.

Weingast, Barry R. 2009. "Second Generation Fiscal Federalism: The Implica-tions of Fiscal Incentives." *Journal of Urban Economics* 65(3):279–293.

Weingast, Barry R. 2014. "Second Generation Fiscal Federalism: Political Aspects of Decentralization and Economic Development." *World Develop-ment* 53:14–25.

Whiting, Susan H. 2000. *Power and Wealth in Rural China: The Political Economy of Institutional Change*. New York: Cambridge University Press.

Wibbels, Erik. 2000. "Federalism and the Politics of Macroeconomic Policy and Performance." *American Journal of Political Science* 44(4):687–702.

Wibbels, Erik. 2001. "Federal Politics and Market Reform in the Developing World." *Studies in Comparative International Development* 36(2):27–53.

Williamson, Oliver. 1975. *Markets and Hierarchies: Analysis and Antitrust Implications, a Study in the Economics of Internal Organization*. New York: Free Press.

Wintrobe, Ronald. 2000. *The Political Economy of Dictatorship*. Cambridge: Cambridge University Press.

Woller, Gary M., and Kerk Phillips. 1998. "Fiscal Decentralisation and IDC Economic Growth: An Empirical Investigation." *The Journal of Develop-ment Studies* 34(4):139–148.

Wong, Christine. 1991. The Maoist "Model" Reconsidered: Local Self-Reliance and the Financing of Rural Industrialization. In *New Perspectives on the Cultural Revolution*, ed. William A. Joseph, Christine Wong, and David Zweig. Cambridge, MA: Harvard University Press, pp. 183–196.

Wong, Christine. 1992. "Fiscal Reform and Local Industrialization: The Problematic Sequencing of Reform in Post-Mao China." *Modern China* 18(2):197–226.

Wong, Christine, Christopher Heady, and Wing Thye Woo. 1995. *Fiscal Management and Economic Reform in the People's Republic of China*. Hong Kong: Oxford University Press.

Wu, Jinglian. 2016. *Dangdai Zhongguo Jingji Gaige Jiaocheng (Understanding and Interpreting China's Economic Reform)*. Shanghai: Shanghai Far East Publishing House.

Wu, Kuo-cheng. 1962. *Reminiscences of Wu Kuo-Cheng: Oral History*. New York: Chinese Oral History Project Collection of Reminiscences at Columbia University.

Wu, Ruo-Yu. 1992. *Zhanhou Taiwan Gongying Shiye zhi Zhengjing Fenxi (A Political Economic Analysis of Post-War Taiwan Public Enterprises)*. Taipei: Yeqiang Publisher.

Wu, Yongping. 2005. *A Political Explanation of Economic Growth: State Survival, Bureaucratic Politics, and Private Enterprises in the Making of Taiwan's Economy, 1950–1985*. Cambridge, MA: Harvard University Asia Center.

Xiang, Huaicheng. 1999. *Zhongguo Caizheng Wushinian (50 Years of Chinese Fiscal Budget)*. Beijing: Zhongguo Caizheng Jingji Chubanshe.

Xiang, Huaicheng, ed. 2006. *Zhongguo Caizheng Tongshi: dangdai juan (The General History of Chinese Finance: the Contemporary Period)*. Beijing: Zhongguo Caizheng Jingji Chubanshe.

Xin, Xiangyang. 2000. *Bainian Boyi: Zhongguo Zhongyang yu Difang Guanxi Yibai Nian (A Hundred Years of Game: 100 Years of Central–Local Relations in China)*. Jinan: Shandong People's Publishing House.

Xu, Chenggang. 2011. "The Fundamental Institutions of China's Reforms and Development." *Journal of Economic Literature* 49(4):1076–1151.

Yang, Dali. 1996. *Calamity and Reform in China: State, Rural Society, and Institutional Change Since the Great Leap Famine*. Stanford: Stanford University Press.

Yang, Dali L. 1997. *Beyond Beijing: Liberalization and the Regions in China*. London: Routledge.

Yang, Dali L. 2004. *Remaking the Chinese Leviathan: Market Transition and the Politics of Governance in China*. Stanford: Stanford University Press.

Yang, Kuisong. 2008. "Reconsidering the Campaign to Suppress Counterrevolutionaries." *The China Quarterly* 193:102–121.

Yeh, Chi-kai. 2007. Jiang Jingguo Wannian Zhengzhi Gaige de Beijing (1975–1988) (The Background of Political Reforms in Chiang Ching-kuo's Later Years: 1975–1988). Master's thesis. National Central University Taipei.

Young, Alwyn. 2000. "The Razor's Edge: Distortions and Incremental Reform in the People's Republic of China." *The Quarterly Journal of Economics* 115(4):1091–1135.

Yu, Chingchun. 2009. Taiwan Jishu Guanliao de Renmai yu Paixi (The Networks and Factions of Taiwan's Economic Technocrats (1949–1988)). Master's thesis. National Chengchi University Taipei.

Zhang, Jun. 2007. "Fenquan yu Zengzhang: Zhongguo de Gushi (Decentralization and Growth: China Context)." *China Economic Quarterly* 7(1):21–51.

Zhang, Qi, Dong Zhang, Mingxing Liu, and Victor Shih. 2021. "Elite Cleavage and the Rise of Capitalism under Authoritarianism: A Tale of Two Provinces in China." *The Journal of Politics* 83(3):1010–1023.

Zhang, Qi, and Mingxing Liu. 2019. *Revolutionary Legacy, Power Structure, and Grassroots Capitalism under the Red Flag in China*. Cambridge: Cambridge University Press.

Zhang, Suhua. 2006. *Bianju: Qiqianren dahui shimo (The Whole Story of the Seven Thousand Cadres Conference)*. Beijing: Zhongguo Qingnian Chubanshe.

Zhao, Dexin, ed. 1989. *Zhonghua Renmin Gongheguo Shi: 1967–1984 (Economic History of the People's Republic of China: 1967–1984)*. Zhengzhou: Henan People's Publishing House.

Zhi, Xiaomin. 2008. *Liu Shaoqi and the Jinsui Land Reform (Liu Shaoqi yu Jinsui tugai)*. Taipei: Xinwei Information Science Press.

Zhou, Enlai. 1984. *Zhou Enlai Xuanji (Selected Works of Zhou Enlai: Volume 2)*. Beijing: Renmin Publishing House.

Zhou, Xueguang. 2022. *The Logic of Governance in China: An Organizational Approach*. Cambridge: Cambridge University Press.

Zhu, Rongji. 2013. *Zhu Rongji on the Record: The Road to Reform 1991–1997*. Washington, DC: Brookings Institution Press.

Cambridge Elements ☰

Chinese Economy and Governance

Luke Qi Zhang
Fudan University

Luke Qi Zhang is Associate Professor at the China Center for Economic Studies of the School of Economics at Fudan University. He specializes in the political economy of authoritarianism generally and how elite politics affects policy making and economic outcomes in China specifically. His book (co-authored with Mingxing Liu) *Revolutionary Legacy, Power Structure, and Grassroots Capitalism under the Red Flag in China* (Cambridge University Press, 2019) proposes a theory of localized property rights protection under authoritarianism, and applies the theory to the private sector development in both the Mao era and the current reform era in China.

Mingxing Liu
Peking University

Mingxing Liu is Professor of the China Institute for Educational Finance Research at Peking University. He works on China's elite politics, economic growth, and local governance. He has published numerous academic articles in international and Chinese journals such as the *American Political Science Review, Comparative Political Studies, Comparative Politics,* and *Journal of Politics*.

Daniel Mattingly
Yale University

Daniel Mattingly is Associate Professor in the Department of Political Science at Yale University. He studies the domestic and international politics of authoritarian regimes, with a focus on China. His book *The Art of Political Control in China* (Cambridge University Press, 2020) received the Best Book Award from the Democracy and Autocracy Section of the American Political Science Association and was named a best book of the year by *Foreign Affairs*.

About the Series
The works in this Elements series examine China's economy, governance, and policy-making process. Members of the political and business communities will find the series a valuable guide to navigate China's complex policy and governance system and understand its business environment.

Cambridge Elements ≡

Chinese Economy and Governance

Elements in the Series

A full series listing is available at: www.cambridge.org/ECEG

Printed in the United States
by Baker & Taylor Publisher Services